"I've had the pleasure of working side by side with Adam Berry over the last fifteen years. Chasing ghosts led to very real, spiritual questions about spirits, the paranormal, and the belief system it actually is. It's no surprise that the enlightenment that followed has led from a curious hobby to this compendium of what the paranormal has to offer to the 'life after death' conversation. The supernatural is deeper and more profound than most realize, and together with many other voices he consulted in the field of paranormal and spiritual research, Adam perfectly encapsulates it here. The next time someone asks you if ghosts are real, hand them this book and say, 'It's so much more than that. Here.'"

—**Amy Bruni,** bestselling author, host of *Haunted Road*
iHeartRadio podcast, co-host of *Kindred Spirits*

"*Goodbye Hello* has arrived at a time when it is needed most, as the world has come to embrace new answers and ask new questions with many turning to the paranormal for insight. Adam Berry eloquently interweaves history, spookiness, and compelling personal experience that reflect our desire to learn more about what it means to be human by looking to those who've lived and passed and most profoundly, continued."

—**Tyler Henry**, psychic medium, star of Netflix's *Life After Death*,
and bestselling author

"Adam Berry has taken the necessary and needed steps to begin meaning-ful, inclusive dialogs that reveal how the fear of Death, feelings of loneliness, and the grieving experience can be used to generate more profound and insightful ideas in helping to explain our seemingly shared existence. In a world brimming with unanswered questions about Life, Death, and the possibility of continued existence after Death, Adam Berry has taken on the essential work of seeking out possible answers, no matter where those answers may be found."

—**John E.L. Tenney**, author, researcher, and one of the most well-recognized
and highly sought-after investigators of UFO, paranormal,
and occult phenomena in the world

"My friend and colleague, Adam Berry, has been investigating the paranormal for many years. In his first book, he shares his belief on what happens after we die based on years of research and experience. He also provides captivating stories and personal interviews that help the living to better understand and make our way through grief and loss. His insights are both compelling and thought provoking. This book is a must read!"

—**Chip Coffey**, psychic, medium, *Kindred Spirits*, star of *Psychic Kids* on A&E

"In *Goodbye Hello, Kindred Spirits*' Adam Berry offers readers a unique and transformative lens through which to view death…and whatever comes next. Through heartwarming anecdotes from leaders in the field and thought-provoking insights gathered over his decades of investigating the unexplained, Berry's *Goodbye Hello* reveals how the paranormal can be a powerful tool for processing grief, offering comfort to those in mourning, advice to the curious, and direction to the seekers."

—**Greg Newkirk**, producer on *Hellier*, paranormal researcher, and museum curator

GOODBYE
HELLO

GOODBYE HELLO

PROCESSING GRIEF
AND UNDERSTANDING DEATH
THROUGH THE PARANORMAL

ADAM BERRY

A REGALO PRESS BOOK

Goodbye Hello:
Processing Grief and Understanding Death through the Paranormal
© 2023 by Adam Berry
All Rights Reserved

ISBN: 979-8-88845-040-6
ISBN (eBook): 979-8-88845-041-3

Cover Design by Cody Corcoran
Author photo by Michael and Susan Karchmer
Interior design and composition by Greg Johnson, Textbook Perfect

As part of the mission of Regalo Press, a donation is being made to The Lily House, as chosen by the author. Find out more about this organization at thelilyhouse.org

Regalo Press
New York ✦ Nashville
regalopress.com

Published in the United States of America
1 2 3 4 5 6 7 8 9 10

For my mom, Sylvia, and dad, Junior,
who love and encourage me in all the right ways.

For my husband, Ben.
My right arm and the best parts of me.
A phrase maker.
I love you.

For Grannie and Mamaw
and those who have gone before, who continue
to find ways to make me see the world differently,
even from the great beyond.

Contents

Introduction

It was just after midnight, and I was standing in the middle of a Gettysburg battlefield. It was early 2006, and I had just split off from the ghost tour I was on that night. Not finding enough ghosts to sate my curiosity, I asked the tour guide if I could walk down to a section of the field that was rumored to be incredibly haunted.

"I wouldn't go alone," he said.

But I was not him. So I left and made my way to the place on the battlefield where people said they saw and heard the most paranormal activity. I was alone in the darkness; after a few moments, I found myself staring at what I can only describe as misty ethereal figures gliding through the depths of the woods.

They looked like humans, but weren't—at least, not exactly—and they were manifesting one by one. The anomalies moved in and out of the trees, their ambient glow appearing and disappearing from my field of vision. Distant sounds of war were all around me: the booms of cannons and the *pop, pop, pop* of musket fire. The noises were muted, but at the same time, seemed like they were right next to me, as though I was hearing the sounds permeating through the darkness. Maybe through time and space.

Then came the screaming.

And the yelling.

I can't remember which was first.

The anguished sounds of death permeated the air—not from the entities I was watching, or from any people at all, but from a battle that had happened almost a century and a half ago.

I probably should have run away, but I stood there, transfixed. I looked to my left, then my right, to see if anyone else was witnessing this strange phenomenon. I looked back to where my tour group had last stopped; there was no one there at all. I was witnessing echoes of an ancient battle unfolding in front of me, and I was completely alone. I took a deep breath, and, with courage manifested somewhere within me, I walked into the line of trees.

That's the story of how I began my journey to the job I have today. But it's not where my story starts.

My name is Adam Berry, and I am a paranormal researcher, investigator, educator, and television personality. I have explored some of the most intensely haunted places in the world on my quest to understand, explain, and come to terms with what happens after we die.

The act of looking for ghosts to document their existence isn't a new concept, but, as I've sought out and found evidence of people remaining in this world after death, I've begun to delve deeper into what ghosts truly are and why they exist.

I've also been asking a question that, to my knowledge, no one has ever seriously explored before: can we use what we know about ghosts, and what we discover through paranormal investigation, to come to terms with our own mortality? Can talking to ghosts help us make peace with death and loss?

I believe it can, and that by exploring what happens after we pass away, we can gain a better understanding of ourselves, our relationships with other people, our fears and insecurities, and our grief, and allow ourselves to better accept the fact of our mortality.

This book is meant to do two things: to explain what I've learned in my career as a paranormal researcher about how death affects us both while we're alive and after we've passed, and to ask broader questions about what we can learn from each other in sharing our experiences.

One of the most impactful conversations I have ever had about death happened at one of my very first paranormal conventions, back in 2011.

These weekend events allowed those interested in the paranormal to gather together in a haunted location, listen to lectures, and then participate in guided investigations. I had just finished a talk on ghosts and our experiences on cases when a lovely woman walked up to me and said, "Can I ask you a question?" I never could have anticipated what she said next.

"I've been given a few weeks to live," she said, "and I want to know how I can communicate with my family and loved ones after I die." I was speechless. If I had thought before that conversation that what we did on TV, or in the paranormal world, was mostly for entertainment, all of those easy and simple ideas about why I did what I did vanished in an instant. Up until that moment, I had been capturing spooky things on camera for the entertainment of the audience, but also my own fun. I knew it intellectually, but I had never truly absorbed the idea that a ghost is an actual person in a different state of being.

I tried to find words that would give her some comfort. While I have theories about how ghosts communicate, it's impossible to instruct someone on how to do it. Also, even though I believe every person has a spiritual energy that survives the death of the body, not everyone becomes a ghost, or returns in some way to communicate with the living. Trying not to cry in front of her, I put my hand on her shoulder and said, "I'm so sorry. I don't know what to say. I wish we knew how ghosts and spirits reach out to the living, but we just don't know."

Her face didn't change. There was no disappointment or sadness. She was already going through one of the hardest things a person could face.

"I wish I could be of more help," I said. "Again, I am so sorry."

"That's okay," she said. "I just want to be able to stay in touch with my family after I have gone. There's still so much I want to see."

I had never experienced this kind of intense conversation with anyone, let alone a stranger. She had come to the event to not find out how to communicate with a ghost, but to learn the art of communication *as* a ghost. Before I lost it completely, I said, "If you do figure it out, after...will you find me and let me know?"

She looked me square in the eyes, her face softened, and she radiated a peaceful understanding I had never seen in anyone before.

"Of course," she said. She took a moment, then she left. I have not heard from her since, but I hope she found what she was looking for.

Paranormal investigation leads to discoveries that allow the living to visualize an existence beyond our own reality. At least personally, it makes me feel like I am connected to something bigger than this life.

Almost every piece of evidence I've ever captured during my investigations has led to more questions, but through it all I've become convinced of one thing: that there is definitely an afterlife. Scientists, paranormal researchers, psychics, and religious scholars all have different ideas about death, ghosts, and the great beyond.

Introduction

I can't explain what definitely happens—I just know there is more to come after we die.

Maybe, one day, the living will have solid answers about what happens during and after death. For now, I am determined to document everything I know, based on my own personal paranormal experiences and what I've learned from other people who seek to unravel the mysteries of the afterlife. I believe that sharing my ideas and experiences is an opportunity to help others gain new insights into coping with loss, as well as processing grief and all that comes with it. Together, we can better understand what happens after we take our last breath, and do our best to dispel the fear and stigma surrounding it.

Up until that moment in Gettysburg, I thought I had figured out where I was heading in life. I had spent my time thus far pursuing my dreams of being on Broadway, graduating in 2005 from the Boston Conservatory with a BFA in musical theater. In fact, the only reason I was in Gettysburg in the first place was to perform with TheaterWorksUSA and secure my Equity card.

I didn't know it at the time, but while I was having the most profound paranormal experience of my life, I was also unlocking something deep within. Soon, I would realize that the spiritual world had much bigger plans for me. That one experience rerouted the trajectory of my life.

I believe all roads lead to where you are meant to be. Looking back to how it all began, it seems like I was the only one who was unaware of what my future would be…at least from a metaphysical standpoint. Now, I have found myself at the crossroads of paranormal exploration and the desire to better understand our own end-of-life experience. I strongly feel we can find comfort in our grief and loss through the theories we share about ghosts and the afterlife. But I want to be clear that they're just that—theories.

Everything I talk about in this book is my opinion, in connection with shared ideas among colleagues, friends, and experts. My most-trusted paranormal colleagues have a mantra: believe everything we are saying and believe none of what we are saying. The point is to make your own connections, create your own ideas, and come to your own conclusions. I hope that by the end of this book, you may have broadened your perspective on what comes next. If you've found your way to this text, whether you're processing your own grief or simply looking to expand your ideas about the paranormal, this is where you are meant to be. Embrace it and enjoy the ride.

PART ONE

Death Is a Part of Life

CHAPTER 1

Death as the Beginning

Everyone who's seen *Kindred Spirits* knows the story of my "first" paranormal experience in Gettysburg, but I'll tell you a secret right now that I've never shared publicly before: I had had paranormal experiences long before that, going as far back as I can remember.

The first time was when I was about eight years old, in our family home in Florence, Alabama. One night, I woke up with a start, hearing what I thought was a dog scratching on the bathroom door just across from my bedroom. The only trouble was, we didn't have a dog.

My bedroom door was open and I could see out into the hallway. No animal was there, but I clearly heard the sound. It went from outside the bathroom, across the hall, and into my bedroom. It was unmistakably a dog. I could hear its little nails on the hardwood floor and the jingling of the tags on its collar.

The sound got louder as it came closer to the foot of my bed, where our old knob-and-tube TV set was sitting. It was the kind that, when you turned it off, it still had a faint glow for a minute or two. At that time of night, it had been off for hours. When whatever was making that noise got close to the TV, a faint glow would appear on the screen, and then dim to black in a weird pulsating rhythm.

After this sequence happened a few times, any grogginess I had from waking up was gone. I was completely, fully awake, the hairs on my arms standing up straight and my skin covered in goosebumps. I even pinched myself to make sure I wasn't dreaming.

Scratch, scratch, scratch, walk, walk, walk. Over and over again. I was scared, really scared. I wanted to run to my parents' room, but I couldn't. I shared the room with my younger brother Lucas and hoped that he was awake so that I would not be alone in this moment, but he was fast asleep. Whatever was making the sound was blocking my exit and I felt trapped.

I'm not sure how I knew what to do, but I knew for sure that I had to handle this situation myself, that no one was going to help me. I sat up straight, gripped the blankets, and in my loudest, most authoritative voice, I yelled "STOP!" And poof, gone. All the sounds stopped at once. No more scratching or jingling, just eerie quiet. A strange calm came over me, and I just laid back down and went to sleep.

That last part of the story is still odd to me. Why, once I was able to leave the room, did I not go to my parents for help? I don't know why I didn't do more in those moments after the ghost dog disappeared. Maybe it was then that my future in the paranormal was sealed. The universe knew more about me and my path than I could have ever imagined.

After that experience, I became much more attuned to strange phenomena in my house. One thing I heard frequently was footsteps going downstairs into the basement. It was an especially creepy basement, with lots of dark corners and ominous crevasses for menacing things to hide in. But we had our laundry down there, so there was often someone using the stairs. However, there were also plenty of other times when I would clearly hear footsteps, and then look up to find my parents sitting totally still in the next room.

My mom remembers me asking her often whether someone had just gone into the basement, because I could have sworn at that time I heard someone descend, or would catch a glimpse of something out of the corner of my eye. Once I started hearing those footsteps, I was convinced the house was haunted.

Though I would listen for those phantom paws, I never heard the ghost dog again—but those seemingly human footsteps happened all the time. I'd wonder, *Why is mom doing laundry this late?* And then have to remind myself that she wasn't, and that it was probably the ghost. I feel like any "normal" child would convince themselves it was their mom and not something unexplained. For some reason, I was comfortable in the ambiguity.

Later in life, I learned I wasn't the only person who thought that house on Bluff Street was haunted. In fact, my parents were warned before they moved in—by Santa Claus.

He wasn't the real Santa, of course, but the man who played him locally every Christmas had lived in our house with his family before we moved in. "His wife was telling us about the house being haunted," my mom recently told me, "but we didn't say anything to you about it. I don't think your dad believed it at the time."

Of course they wouldn't believe it. That's how every good horror story starts, doesn't it? They were a young couple ready to start a family and needed a rental they could afford. When I was talking to my parents about the hauntings in that house for this book, I asked my dad if he had any paranormal experiences there.

"I could have," he said, "but you know, I really didn't pay any attention to it."

It makes sense, though. They were a couple in their early thirties who both had full-time jobs and were focused on their family, not ghosts. They had no time for distractions and didn't need the added worry of a haunted house.

"The way I remember," my dad said, "was prior to us moving into there, we went to a party on a Friday night and [the previous owners] were talking about it. They said they were going to move and buy a house and we told them that we wanted to rent the one they were living in."

"If I'm not mistaken," he continued, "it was then that they said something about 'Well, you're gonna have to put up with it.' I think they called the ghost Gertrude."

The family then went on to recount the time that they had come home to find that the giant mirror on the wall behind the dresser had been moved ten feet away from where it was secured, but everything that was on the dresser was still in place, none of the perfume bottles or jewelry boxes disturbed from where they had been before the mirror was moved.

Let's pause for a minute here. Because my father heard this story and didn't even flinch. He was told point blank about some crazy supernatural activity, and instead of saying, "No thank you, I'll find a house that isn't haunted," he moved his family right into Gertrude's house. That is badass.

When he told me that story, I was shocked. It rivals some of the claims we've gotten on *Kindred Spirits*, but my parents had never told me about it before. I've always said I had no control over where I am today, doing what I do in the paranormal field. Looking back—and hearing stories like this—it just makes sense.

My dad might not remember experiencing anything strange in the house on Bluff Street, but my mom had a different take on it. "Well, things started going missing in the bathroom," she told me. "A lot of makeup and female things would just go missing."

This is a common occurrence in houses that are haunted— things unexpectedly disappear. You put something down and when you go back to get it a minute later, it's nowhere to be seen. The thing could show up again in the same spot a few minutes later, or somewhere that doesn't make any sense at all. Once, a client on a case told me that her keys would often go missing. One day, frustrated, she yelled, "Please, I need my car keys, I have to go to work." Then her keys dropped from the ceiling, right through a ceiling fan at the highest speed, and hit the ground.

I have theories as to why spirits do things like taking away objects you need. One thought is because they want to get your attention, or they want to mess with you. In my mother's case, I think Gertrude liked her makeup. When things like that started happening to her, my mom reconsidered what the previous tenants had said, about there being a female ghost in the house.

"I don't know if it was just because of the vibes in that house," she told me, "but when you started talking about hearing dogs running around, I thought, *Well, I guess it is haunted.*"

I was living in a real haunted house, but there was a lot more around me that was spooky. As a child of the late '80s and early '90s, I was surrounded by truly excellent paranormal pop culture, from Stephen King and R. L. Stine novels to movies like *Ghostbusters* and *Beetlejuice*. These books and movies not only piqued my young curiosity, but also opened up new ideas about what is actually out there after we die. Yes, Hollywood exaggerates its stories for entertainment's sake, but most good stories are rooted in some kind of factual experience. So, did a scary clown live in a sewer at the end of my street? I didn't know for sure, but it was a burning question that my spooky little mind needed to figure out.

The last experience I ever had in the house on Bluff Street was on the day we were moving out. I was ten years old, sitting in the passenger seat of the U-Haul, helping Uncle Charlie back down our sloped gravel driveway. He asked me to look out the window to make sure he wasn't going to back into the tree in the corner of the yard.

I gave him the all-clear, then turned around to see that all of the shutters on the house were closed, covering the windows. I turned around to check the driveway again, and when I looked back at the house a second time, they were all open and back to where they should be. The thing is, though, the shutters were all decorative. They had never closed and weren't made to do so—yet they had closed, at least for me. It was as if the house had one final trick up its sleeve, a way to say goodbye and good luck, all in the same moment. A wink to say, "Don't forget me."

Believe me, I haven't. I'd love to visit that house again one day just so we could have one more conversation. I wonder if Gertrude thinks about me as much as I think about her.

Once we moved away, into our new good-school-district rambler, I put those ghosts out of my mind. I was more focused on performing, learning other skills like public speaking that would serve me well. I still had a thing for scary books, movies, and haunted houses, but my goal was to be on Broadway. It took that life-changing experience in Gettysburg to get back the piece of myself I left behind on Bluff Street. Once it happened, I was all in. Those unexplained childhood moments came back in a flurry, and all of a sudden, I was headed on a path into the unknown.

CHAPTER 2

Death as a Way of Life

After my experience in Gettysburg, I became fairly confident that ghosts exist. That didn't mean I had any idea what to do with that information. Until that moment, when I felt the presence of the dead, I'd had very little experience with death in my life.

When I was four, my grandfather, Athel Guy Berry Sr., lost his battle with cancer. My pawpaw was a Purple Heart veteran of World War II who loved his family, and we loved him right back. Even though I was very young, I still have strong memories of his visitation service, including a debate between my parents about whether I should be allowed to see him in his casket. My mother was afraid it would be too much for someone so young, but my father reasoned that I had as much right to say goodbye as anyone else.

My parents could have chosen to shield me from this experience. Instead, they saw it as an opportunity to share in the moment together as a family. I was sad, but I think it was because everyone else was sad. I didn't understand the connection between the grief of a loved one and the emotion of sadness. Everyone was having a shared experience, and I was part of it. Being with family made it less scary and confusing. If we faced it as a group, we were stronger together.

I remember adults looking at me, waiting to see what kind of reaction I might have. Then, my father lifted me in his arms, and there laid out before me was my pawpaw. He was in a suit with his hands gently placed on his lap. To me, it looked like he was sleeping. From what I understood, even at four years old, my pawpaw had gone to be with God and live in Heaven. Everyone was saying that, at any rate. I was taught a very specific biblical idea of the afterlife, and, while my views are different today, it was a foundation that allowed me to comprehend what was happening.

I think at this early age, being exposed to death and connecting it to faith made it less scary than it could have been. I knew I would see him again someday, so to me it wasn't goodbye but rather "until we meet again."

Once I met some ghosts, and realized that people who had passed could still be present on this plane, I started to really think about the afterlife—what it means, and why we'd even want to try to communicate with spirits in the first place.

I had spent many hours in libraries when I was young, checking out books on ghosts and haunting stories. Among books like *Scary Stories to Tell in the Dark*, I would occasionally stumble across more thought-provoking, nonfiction books about the paranormal by authors like Hans Holzer. Even though I was twenty-two when I had that battlefield encounter, I found myself going back to a childhood favorite: a nonfiction book called *Thirteen Alabama Ghosts and Jeffrey* by Kathryn Tucker Windham and Margaret Gillis Figh. It told stories of real paranormal encounters in the place I grew up.

Those weren't just "once upon a time" scary stories, they were—at least to the best of my knowledge—accounts of things that really happened.

Back then, I was thirsting for real proof of paranormal activity and a better understanding of what I had seen and felt. At that point, it hadn't crossed my mind that you could intentionally investigate ghosts at all, let alone with a group of like-minded individuals with the goal of documenting tangible activity. And I assumed that for any spirit encounter, I had to be in the right place at the right time.

That is, until one winter when I moved to Cape Cod with my then-boyfriend, now husband, Ben.

Ben and I fell for each other very quickly, just as we were getting out of college. He was a classically trained actor from the University of Minnesota Guthrie, and studied Shakespeare at the Globe and National Theater in London. At the Boston Conservatory, I studied lyrics and scores, focusing on singing, vocal techniques, and different styles of music. To us those were two entirely different worlds—but I love a good classic theater piece, and Ben loves musicals just as much as I do, and boy can he sing! It was a match made in heaven.

Besides a shared love of theater, we also both loved all things frightening: movies, books, haunted houses, ghosts, Halloween, graveyards...the list goes on and on. We both, as kids, built haunted houses in our homes and forced our friends to participate in the scares. It only made sense that we'd meet and fall in love in one of the oldest, spookiest places either of us had ever been.

Cape Cod juts out into the Atlantic Ocean like an arm, curling in to form a bay, with the tip flicking inward like a crooked fingernail. At that very farthest point of Massachusetts is a tiny fishing village called Provincetown.

This area of the globe is magical—I mean real, actual magic. Some say the curve of the land creates a vortex to the supernatural. Your history books may want you to believe that the Pilgrims landed at Plymouth, but in reality, those colonists first landed in Provincetown in 1620, docking the Mayflower in the safety of Provincetown harbor. I don't think that was a coincidence. I think they were drawn here like sailors to a siren, fixated on the land's beauty. When I arrived, I immediately felt like I belonged, and that I wanted to be fully engulfed by the energy of this town.

"No matter how you think about Provincetown, it's an end point," Ben said. "It's where people come to gather and where they all have something to do, whether it be vacationing or doing something creative or figuring out what's next in their life. They come here to experience a new form of energy. It's full of this vibrant, ever-changing atmosphere that they're able to tap in to. That's what makes it magical."

When we landed in Provincetown, thousands of miles away from our respective homes, it was the perfect place for Ben and me to connect, not just with each other but with our love of the supernatural. Spiritually, there is more to this area than unshakable feelings. The National Park Service has found Paleoindian artifacts on the outer Cape that indicate human habitation dating back more than 10,000 years. In recorded history, the town is rich with countless stories of shipwrecks, mooncussers, and murders, leaving behind traces of sea captains, widows, warriors, and mischief makers. Some of the antique homes here were "floated" to town from the extreme outermost end of the Cape, a place called Hell Town, a smaller whaling community of the 1800s which granted easy access to the sea. Legends say that mooncussers in Hell Town would cause nighttime shipwrecks using strategically-placed lanterns on shore, then board the vessels to loot and plunder, leaving no survivors. The energy of it all soaks into the very soil and permeates the sturdy walls of the oldest houses on the Cape.

Provincetown was also the first place where I experienced the death of a friend as an adult. At that point, any separation I had between sadness and grief disappeared. It was the realization that someone I knew, and saw all the time, was here yesterday and then suddenly was gone. But were they gone forever?

My friend John Pacheco, who is also no longer with us now, once had an experience that demonstrated to me that ghosts weren't just spirits from the past.

We had a mutual friend, Lynn, who was John's roommate at the time. One morning around 5:30 a.m., he heard her outside of his bedroom window, as if she were talking on the phone. She was saying, "I have to go on a trip, but I will be fine. I'm okay." When John recalled the story to me, he told me that at that moment, he thought to himself, "*It's so early. I wonder where she's going.* She hadn't said anything to me about it." He went back to sleep and around 9:00 a.m. he woke up and started his usual morning routine.

When he went to the kitchen, he noticed that her bedroom door was closed and thought it odd. She was an early riser and was always awake before him, having made coffee and started her day. He waited another hour before gently knocking on the bedroom door to see if she was still asleep or even in the apartment. When he didn't get a response, he opened the door and discovered that she had died. The autopsy revealed that she had passed away, from a heart condition, during the night. When I first heard this story I was shocked: Lynn had communicated with John as a ghost almost immediately after she left this earth.

This story gave me, John, and her group of friends comfort. She said it herself: "I will be fine. I'm okay." It was a final message to convey that she was going on a journey and would be all right. It was the first time I realized a ghost could be someone you know, not just a legend. It was at this point that I wanted to start looking for ghosts and seeing who else was out there.

It was very easy to get access to old and historic properties in Provincetown in the off-season. Once the summer tourists cleared out, our friends would move in, usually subletting grand, classic Cape Cod homes that were old and full of stories. Owners would charge lower rents in exchange for tenants acting as caretakers— kind of like *The Shining*, but in real life, and happening all over town.

It was in these locations where I began my journey into paranormal research, honing my investigation and communication skills. Ben and I had seen a handful of *Ghost Hunters* episodes by this point, and we were utterly fascinated by the idea that you could "hunt" for supernatural phenomena. We had one piece of equipment—an audio recorder—and we would sit for hours in the dark, asking questions to possible entities to capture electronic voice phenomena (EVP), which is when a recording device picks up a voice you can't hear with your ears, theoretically a ghost's.

Ben, myself, and others would visit friends in these Cape Cod rentals and sit around in the dark asking basic questions: "Are you there?," "How old are you?," "Can you make a noise for us?" In the winter of 2008, a friend of ours was renting one of the oldest houses in town. The rumor I had always heard was that there was a body buried under or very near to the foundation.

The legends go back so far that in 1936, the local newspaper referred to the house as "haunted" in an article. I've also read that one of the previous owners, who did some renovations and repairs, was told by the contractor to not close up a crack at the base of the fireplace because "that's where the spirits come and go."

Walking up to the Colonial-style house, with its dark red siding and small windows that resembled eyes staring out into the world,

I could just feel a shift in the environment. Once we arrived, I set out to look for the tombstone said to mark the spot. Walking around to the front of the house, I noticed something in the stone foundation among other large rocks and boulders. If you weren't looking for it you would miss it, but there, half-buried in the earth as if it was gasping for its last breath before sinking into the soil, was a small headstone. Time was not kind to the epitaph, and I couldn't make out what it said. A name? Perhaps a date? Whatever it said, it didn't matter. The folklore was real, and it gave me so much hope that we would get some sort of paranormal activity once we started searching.

You have to understand that my perspective then was totally different from my approach to investigation today. At that early point in my journey, I wanted experiences. That's it. I wanted to see or hear a ghost. I wanted to capture evidence. To me, that gravestone was so exciting—and maybe a sign of activity to come—but I hadn't yet connected to the human aspect of that object. I didn't think about the once-living person that stone represented.

But now, those are the questions that have become my primary goal in my work. Who are the people who stay behind? Do they choose to remain on Earth? Are they here all the time? What does our world look like to someone who has passed on? And what is *their* world like? These are questions about the mysteries of life that can only be answered by those who have passed on. Having a better understanding of who we are connecting with on the other side changed my entire mission. We can learn from each other.

Not having that deep-rooted idea to guide my path, I was really focused on the fun of it rather than the work. I was trying to recapture the feelings I had in Gettysburg. My mindset has changed since then, but some people prefer to simply seek out experiences and not—like we do now on *Kindred Spirits*—connect to the lives of the spirits left behind. It's not a bad thing; we all learn and grow into our own methods in this field. At that point, I had some growing to do for sure.

Once we entered the house, we headed to the upstairs bedroom with our recorder to conduct an EVP session. When you first start investigating, everything is so fascinating and new. I distinctly remember how cold it was in that unused bedroom. It made the whole experience creepy, ghostly even. In my mind, the space was already haunted. There was no wait-and-see-from-the-evidence attitude.

While investigating, the room was so quiet and still. You could've heard a pin drop between our questions about the headstone, the house, who the spirits were, when they died. When we played back the recorder, we didn't get much. I think we got a "hello," which we all geeked out about, but my ear wasn't as trained then in the art of listening back for evidence, so any words had to be pretty obvious for me to make them out.

During another round of questions, I asked why they were still there in the house, but didn't get any response. I figured it might have something to do with the stone outside, but I couldn't get any solid answers. That simple "hello" was an acknowledgment that whoever was there could interact with us, but actually getting answers from the ghost was another matter. I didn't know it at the time, but I was probably not asking the right questions to really connect with that spirit. Still, I was satisfied with what I had experienced. It wasn't much, but it was something.

These moments were the best part of our off-season routine. My summers were filled with work, doing theater productions and singing at countless venues with a strict focus on making enough money to support us in the winter. The off-season was the time to regroup and heal from the busy summer; for Ben and me, it was an opportunity to dive into the unknown and enjoy a weird passion we didn't think a lot of people shared. One evening while we were watching the newest episode of *Ghost Hunters*, I caught a commercial that said, "Do you have what it takes to be a ghost hunter?"

I didn't hesitate. I immediately thought, *Of course I do!* For me, it wasn't about being on television, it was about being able to investigate ghosts with a professional team and learn a few things in the process. The real appeal was being able to explore on a grand scale, with professional equipment and access to the amazing haunted locations they visited on the show.

My dad always says, "If you don't try you never know," so I tried. The following day I headed to our local internet café and logged on to the Syfy Channel website (back then it was still SciFi) to fill out an application that asked everything from name, age, and location to experiences, beliefs, and fears.

A few months went by and after what felt like an eternity I was shocked to finally get a call! They set up a meeting with one of the producers for a new TV show tentatively called *Ghost Hunters Academy*, which centered on "cadets" who were taught the ways of The Atlantic Paranormal Society (TAPS), the paranormal team behind *Ghost Hunters*. The cadets were tested on knowledge, observed in action, and at the end of the season someone would "graduate" to join TAPS on television.

Sadly, I wasn't chosen to participate in the show's first season. They mentioned that if a replacement for a cadet was needed during filming they would reach out, but that didn't happen. In January of 2010, my phone rang. It was a producer from *Ghost Hunters Academy* saying that they were going to do another season. This time, they wanted my full involvement. No last-minute replacement. The start date would be sometime in February. This new season would be different and more challenging; not all the cadets would make it to the end. Each investigation would have a review by *Ghost Hunters'* Steve Gonsalves, Dave Tango, and Jason Hawes, where one participant would be dismissed. The winner of this competition would get a chance to join *Ghost Hunters* for some upcoming cases.

I was so thrilled to embark on this experience, getting to visit some of the most haunted places in the country. We weren't allowed to know where we were going until we actually got there, but from what the organizers and producers were saying, it sounded like we were in for an unforgettable ride. I was so ready for it.

After some frustrating delays, the producers finally called me with the details—I was to fly to Louisville, Kentucky, the next day and be prepared for multiple weeks on the road, in different climates. That night I scrambled to get everything together that I needed for the trip. In the morning I headed to the airport, caught my flight, and, within an hour of arriving in Louisville, I was wearing thermals and layers of *GHA* swag, and being thrust into my very first professional investigation at Waverly Hills Sanatorium.

Ghost Hunters Academy was a life-changing, but very difficult experience. My first impression of Steve, Dave, and Jay was pure intimidation. I had seen these three on my TV doing something that I wanted to be really good at, and suddenly here I was getting a chance to learn from them. It was overwhelming at first, but I now realize that all the pressure was part of the learning experience itself.

The one thing I quickly became aware of was that I was not in control of who was going to win, regardless of trying my absolute best to do everything correctly. This was a reality television competition. Even if I were the best choice throughout the entire season, if the producers didn't want me to win, I wouldn't.

Sometimes I wanted to give up, just out of pure frustration from the uncertainty. Eventually, I realized I needed to let go of the desire to win. I think that helped me a lot. I was content with the idea that whatever was going to happen in the end, was going to happen. From that point on I was able to relax and be myself. I spoke my mind freely and made sure I was the loudest voice in the room when I needed to be, but I also knew when to keep my mouth shut. I learned everything I possibly could and tried to build upon each new piece of knowledge and advice in a way that set me apart from everyone else.

I was glad to have an opportunity to get better at something that brought me so much joy. During a case at the Mark Twain House in Hartford, Connecticut, I became more brave about approaching Steve and Dave. Steve took note.

"I remember I was talking to another cadet about a paranormal theory," Steve said, "and you came up to me and said, 'Hey, man, I heard a little bit of what you were saying there, but I would really like to understand it better.' I thought that was awesome. You weren't doing it to look better. You were just confident."

I believe another thing that set me apart on *Ghost Hunters Academy* was that I had a knack for putting myself in the mind-set of the spirits we were trying to communicate with. All those years of theater training paid off. I felt that if I embodied the world of the entity and created a scenario they would be drawn to—by thinking about what they would want to talk about, using familiar words or phrases they would know, or playing music they may have been aware of—I would get more responses. If you haven't seen my season of *GHA*, spoiler alert: I won. I was welcomed into a world few have had the privilege of experiencing. I had officially arrived at the start of the next chapter in my life.

My prize for winning *Ghost Hunters Academy* was that I got to participate in six episodes of *Ghost Hunters*. I was awarded the opportunity to travel and work side by side with people I admired. I didn't know it then, but the feeling was mutual—at least a little bit.

"If I'm going to be with somebody for that amount of time, per-sonally, I have to get along with them," Steve told me recently. "I need to like them. I need to trust them. I need to love them as a person and really connect, because you need that trust in the field. I could sense a lot of those things in you. Six episodes doesn't sound like much, but, you know, that could be six months. That could be quite a long time to spend with somebody."

His instincts about me fitting in proved to be right because I ended up spending the better part of four years on the road with Steve.

Getting the opportunity to film six episodes of *Ghost Hunters* was a fabulous prize, but I always joke that my real prize was con-necting with my best friend and paranormal investigation partner, Amy Bruni. We were paired up on my first case with TAPS, and our worlds haven't been the same since. We connected immediately. Our energy worked together, and we started getting activity almost as soon as we began investigating. We felt the same drive to connect with the afterlife, treating each spirit interaction with compassion-ate empathy. Together, we developed new theories through practice.

I was making a living investigating the paranormal. My passion and hobby had suddenly become a career.

CHAPTER 3

The Leap Into the Unknown

On August 22, 2010, Ben and I packed up our old station wagon and headed to Providence, RI. The following day I was to begin filming the episodes of *Ghost Hunters* I had earned from winning *GHA*. After getting settled into my hotel room—and saying another tearful goodbye to Ben—I headed down to the restaurant to join everyone for dinner. I was feeling a mixture of nerves and excitement. On one hand, I felt like I deserved to be there, but on the other, I was an outsider joining a family that had worked together for years.

Rounding the corner into the private area of the restaurant, I was greeted by familiar faces: Kris Williams, Britt Griffith, and Amy Bruni. I had seen all of them on TV, so it was almost as if I had already met them. Steve and Dave were the first out of their seats to give me a warm welcome. After having spent time with them over the course of a few months and being picked by them to join the team, their greeting felt as if we were already old friends.

"My first impression of you was that we would get along," Amy told me, as we were thinking back on those first days. "We instantly started chatting and bonding. I think we hit it off quickly because we wanted the same things out of traveling with a TV show. We clearly love the paranormal, but neither of us is one to sit in the hotel all day when we have a day off. We were constantly hitting up local museums, amazing restaurants, going shopping, or to the spa."

While I was mentally preparing for my first *Ghost Hunters* case as an "investigator in training," which was the Old Stone Fort in Schoharie, New York, I was so glad to have Amy as my investigating partner. Right before we went in, I remember her telling me to follow her lead. "It's easy once you get the hang of it," she told me.

And there was a *lot* to get the hang of. Even just the setup was more intense than it had been on *GHA*: placing cameras in the correct spots and making sure they work, setting up charging stations, learning how to keep track of which ghost gear goes with each pair of investigators, the list goes on and on. The hardest thing, going into that shoot, was putting it out of my mind that I was making a reality TV show and millions of people were going to watch it.

On top of all of those factors, there is another element you can't control: the people you're investigating with, and what they're planning to do. Everyone has their own way of investigating. This can be challenging. I truly believe that energies can mesh, creating an environment to promote clear and sometimes easy communication with the non-living. When those energies don't mesh, I've seen it kill any activity and experiences in the space. It becomes what we call, funnily enough, dead.

"During our first investigation, I remember there not being any tension," Amy recalled. "I had gone years on the show with marked tension, always concerned about what I said and when I said it, down to where I stood in the acknowledged 'line up' of seniority."

I didn't know it then, but she and I were feeling similar things at my first shoot.

"That all went away that day," she added. "You and I investigated, we relaxed, we had great chemistry, and truly enjoyed our time doing what we love. Afterward, I remember the camera operator putting down his camera and saying, 'You guys, this is great. This is just great.' I think they all felt it. It was something new and different."

Our first "run" was in a very large section of the museum that was all glass cases and exhibits. I followed Amy to the far side of the room where we had the best vantage point.

At this stage of my journey, I just wanted to get it right. I didn't want to let anyone down—not the team or the crew I was working with, not the millions of fans who would be watching the show, and not myself. We had one major goal when working on *Ghost Hunters*, to have paranormal experiences that were real and true, and to capture evidence as proof that the activity was happening.

We would try to find natural causes for these experiences first. If we couldn't, we would delve into the paranormal possibilities of what could be going on. Amy and I felt comfortable sharing ideas and theories with each other, even if they were totally off the wall, without fear of judgment or failure. What this formula did was allow us to be ourselves and make mistakes. We could relax and embrace moments of levity. Life on the road is very hard, and we found joy in what we did.

I never took it for granted that our team was allowed access to some of the most incredible and historically significant locations in the country. We were allowed by the US military to investigate battleships, active military bases, and the hallowed ground of Pearl Harbor. In these locations, I had the freedom to open myself up to every experience imaginable. It felt like, in just one year, I had access to more paranormal experiences than I would have had in a decade of investigating on my own.

Back in my early days of *Ghost Hunters* I had no idea how serious it could be, because I was focusing on having experiences for selfish reasons, not trying to understand what was going on behind that experience. That's all part of the growing process, in pretty much everything you do. Pushing your own limits allows you to grow, and that's exactly what I needed to do. But you need a support system to do that, and I had found that in my friendship with Amy.

Once we had established our groove and were working together smoothly as a team, Amy and I felt things gradually shifting, moving beyond just trying to have paranormal experiences. Instead of simply observing what was happening, we wanted to figure out why it was happening, and who was making it happen. We were starting to humanize the spirits we were investigating in a way we hadn't before.

After a few years on *Ghost Hunters*, I started to ask myself tough questions. I could feel the cracks forming in what I believed was my purpose in life. At some point, it really hit me that I only have one life to live. The heaviness of being around death and talking about death all the time—combined with the wear and tear of life on the road—was starting to weigh on me.

But I was learning from all of that, too. Being gone from my family for months on end, missing birthday celebrations and milestones, was harder than I could have imagined. Human beings thrive off of familiar human connection. What I was learning from my experience on the road and our investigations is that just because you are a ghost doesn't mean you lose the desire for human connection. That is the key, especially when you start to really think about what a ghost is: someone who was once alive like you and me, who still has thoughts and emotions, and who most likely still desires some sort of human connection.

The first time I ever truly humanized a ghost was when Amy and I were investigating a courthouse in Georgia for *Ghost Hunters*. People who worked there had many experiences over the years. Their major concern was that an officer had been killed on the courthouse steps, and they thought he might be the one causing the rampant activity. They wanted to know if this person, after his traumatic death, was at peace.

The case started out like any other. We arrived, toured the location with the client, and set up all the gear, then it was time for lights out. I don't know if Amy and I were in the right place at the right time or if the spirits had other plans for us, but this investigation was different. We spent a lot of the time trying to connect to the police officer, without much success. Eventually, we found ourselves in a room with several typewriters on display. Though we weren't reaching the officer, we didn't want to give up making contact with someone. For whatever reason, we started asking "yes" or "no" questions in that particular room, and we were getting results that were surprising. Someone was answering our questions very clearly.

Amy and I shifted our focus to objects in the room, asking this man if the typewriters had belonged to him. Slowly but surely, we determined he had owned one of them. We looked a bit closer at the display. There was a little card that mentioned a particular person who was associated with at least one of these typewriters. There was even a photograph of him.

We did a little internet search and found out that this man was actually the architect of the courthouse. Our world opened up immediately, powered by the research we were able to do on the spot from our phones. There wasn't time to show it on the episode, but we started asking him many questions about his life—whether he was the architect, and how many children he had. To our shock, the man answered…correctly.

At this point Amy had pulled up a biography on the architect of the building and we used this research to inform our questions. We discovered that this architect was so renowned that there was an entire archive in Atlanta that housed all of his materials and sketches. If we had our choice we would have gone to Atlanta, pulled more research, and returned with further documentation to discover more about this person, and, at the simplest level, try to find out why he was lingering.

We had to be content, for the moment, with what we had accomplished. The format of the show didn't allow us to get real closure, but I have a few ideas about why he might have stayed behind. He was a famous architect and this building was one of his greatest accomplishments, so he could have been there to watch over his work. Another theory is that his energy could be attached to the objects he had used to create his masterpiece; when we started interacting with him, bringing up his tools and facts about his life, he was validated and recognized.

Amy and I had made a deeper human connection with someone who had passed. We were trying to understand who this non-living entity was as a person, not just as a conduit of paranormal activity. This gave me a different perspective on what I was doing and why I was investigating. And it was much more fulfilling. We started to humanize who we were speaking with. Those paranormal knocks and bangs are spooky, yes, but the action behind it is familiar. I hadn't made the full connection before that that it was created by a *person*, not just a ghost.

It was the start of my true study of what a ghost is, and the deeper meaning behind who they are and why they are here. That investigation was the jolt of energy I needed to help me start to fill the cracks in my purpose and why I wanted to continue to seek answers. Finding more depth and truth in what we were doing slowly became our major focus. We were already unknowingly opening up to the next step in the way we wanted to affect the supernatural world. We just needed a bit more time to embrace that challenge.

CHAPTER 4

Help in Life and the Afterlife

I have an affinity for cemeteries and graveyards. The mystery and magic of these sacred spaces do something to me that I cannot quite explain. Each headstone or tomb casts deep shadows onto others who rest nearby—bodies and spirits who connect above and below, quite literally, in the earth and in the realm of ghosts. The stones each tell a story and give us a small glimpse into who those people were, with intricate carvings telling us their complete name, how old they lived to be, and sometimes who they were married to and if they had children. Each piece of limestone or marble is a small, albeit incomplete, biography of a life once lived.

Walking through one of these peaceful places, a stillness sets in and makes me contemplate all the mysteries of life and death. In these moments, surrounded by the dead, I am always thinking, *Who are you?* A stone draws my attention and I immediately want to know more. Instantly this person, who might have died hundreds of years ago, is alive in my mind.

There is a saying that you actually die two deaths: your actual death, when you leave this mortal world, and then a second death when no one says your name ever again. I've also heard it said that it only takes three generations to be forgotten forever. So, when I visit a cemetery (especially my favorite, which is old and set back into the woods about a mile and a half so I'm probably the only visitor at this point), I like to spend time bringing the dead back to life.

I say their name, read their epitaph, and try to communicate with them about their wants and needs. I ask if they are okay, and acknowledge their life and the times they lived in. I try to bring up historic events that happened while they were on this earth in living form, to hopefully make a connection or spark some sort of conversation. While I may not have a recorder on me to do in-depth investigation, I always feel a strong urge to try and bring some sort of balance or deeper peace to a human being who has long been forgotten.

While I now believe that the spirit of someone who has passed, if they still remain on earth, likely won't be hanging around their grave waiting for some unsuspecting passersby to disturb their peace, I do think that we can sometimes conjure them back into existence. Or, at least, imbue their spirit with our positive intentions and make it easier for them to connect.

It was in one of these beautifully haunting locations that I captured evidence of something that I never could have expected. Early on in my investigation journey, I would spend a lot of time in old public cemeteries. These locations were easy to access, and provided an opportunity to take a recorder, ask questions of the dead, and see if anyone would respond. Most cemeteries aren't accessible at night, but there was one that I would visit in Provincetown that had a public street running right through its middle, so being in the area at night wasn't against any posted rules. There were grave markers of different shapes and heights, with some leaning at odd angles. Time had taken its toll on a lot of the stones; some had lost their markings and were being overtaken by nature, making it impossible to read their names, learn their story, and bring those buried beneath back to this world.

In the middle of all of this beautiful chaos was a sloping hill with a long set of tombs and crypts that were like mansions for the dead. It was my favorite place to sit and think, looking at the stones below and pondering what it would mean to actually have a place there.

As grand as the mausoleums looked, when I got closer, I would see their true nature. The tombs were decaying to the point where I could see into private sacred spaces. Some doors to these tombs were simply iron gates. All it took was a flashlight and morbid curiosity and you could see the mysteries hidden inside.

One night Ben, two friends, and I decided to take a late walk through the cemetery. I brought my recorder and headed straight for the crypts. Rounding the far side of the long row, there was the most ominous and intriguing set of copper doors I had ever seen, marking a prominent ancestral family. The entrance was like that of an ancient castle, peaked at the top, with rich design inlays and patinated embellishments.

I pressed record. Maybe someone wanted to say something to me. I paused, took a breath, and knocked on the giant door.

"Hello, anyone there?" I asked. Another pause and another knock. "Hello? Helloooooooooo?"

If the dead weren't awake before that, they were definitely awake then. I stopped the recorder and played it back. An EVP (electronic voice phenomena, or an unexplained voice captured on an audio recording) only occurs when you play back the recorder and hear a response you didn't hear when you were talking. I listened.

"Hello? Hellooooooooooo?"

"HELP ME," a voice said.

It was a clear, gentle voice, which seemed sad, maybe even desperate. It sounded as if someone had waited an eternity to say those two words. I was conflicted. On one hand, I was so thrilled that I was able to make contact. On the other hand, it wasn't what I expected at all, which was something like a "hello" back. I'd even take a "go away." In this moment my mind opened up a little more to the world of the afterlife. "HELP ME." Those two words instantly made me realize that there was clearly more than casual communication when it comes to connecting with spirits.

Ben, thinking back on that moment today, said, "It was the most exciting thing. When we actually heard an answer on the recorder, it was confirmation for me. There was undeniable evidence: I was there, I knew that none of us who were alive had said anything after the knocking and you saying hello. It spurred us to look into the history of that mausoleum and learn more about the family. We found out we were friends with their descendants. It was the first inkling of what you are doing now."

The reality is that we have no control over how those who have gone before us will choose to communicate, especially if the non-living are on this mortal plane for a specific purpose.

Getting an EVP that said "Help me" isn't what I had in mind at all, so, for that moment, I put aside the uncomfortable idea that something might have been wrong in their spiritual world. I focused on the excitement of making contact, and got what I wanted without giving anything in return. It was a selfish endeavor I am so glad to have outgrown. However, it would take a few more experiences along these same lines to fully form the ideas and beliefs I have today.

In the fall of 2011, *Ghost Hunters* was set to film at Waverly Hills Sanatorium in Louisville, Kentucky. Once a state-of-the-art tuberculosis hospital that housed upwards of four hundred patients at a time during the worst of the tuberculosis epidemic, Waverly was built in 1926 and is now abandoned. It is widely known in the paranormal community to be one of the most haunted sites in America.

I couldn't have been more excited to go back. I had just hit my one year anniversary on the show—almost two years from the start of *Ghost Hunters Academy*—and Waverly was a homecoming for me. Pulling up to the case as a member of *Ghost Hunters* brought an overwhelming sense of accomplishment. I held my head a little bit higher knowing that this time around I belonged, and didn't have to prove anything to anyone.

I was about to explore this very haunted place with Amy, and we could do anything we wanted to. I wanted to see "the crawler," a dark shadow figure that would climb on walls and down long corridors like a spider. I had even heard stories that you could look down long hallways and see a trash barrel at the far end—but as you approached, what you thought was a barrel would stand up and run directly at you.

Even more exciting: the owners had recently opened a new area of the sanatorium—the nurse's wing. From what I was told, this area had been sealed off for quite some time, and we were going to be the first group to investigate that area. To explore an untouched area of one of the most actively haunted places on Earth is a paranormal investigator's dream come true.

Opening the once-boarded door to where the nurses lived, I had chills all over. As an investigator, I've learned to pay attention to that kind of response. Sometimes your skin reacts before you even have time to think. I knew instinctively that someone was there with us, and I had a feeling those spirits were just as aware.

That long hallway seemed to go on forever. It was so dark you could barely see anything. We used our flashlights to make our way to the main part of the nurse's wing; we like to start in the central area of a large space so we can assess where sounds are coming from more easily. Since this was a section with long hallways on either side and a small room in the middle, we could cover our bases with one person looking down one hallway and the other taking the opposite view. This was important because the owners had experiences in that area specifically relating to tapping and knocking, so we wanted to make sure we knew where the sounds might be coming from.

If you've seen that episode of *Ghost Hunters*, you've only seen a fraction of what happened that night. We started off as we normally do, by introducing ourselves. We asked for the spirits' names, and whether they had worked at the hospital or were patients. Out of nowhere, we heard a small tap a few yards down the hallway. Amy and I looked at each other.

"Can you do that again?" she asked.

There was a louder tap on the opposite side of the hallway in which we were standing. Our heads jerked around so fast they could have popped off if they weren't attached. We explained to whoever was listening that we didn't want them to perform for us, but that when they interacted on command like that, it let us know that they really were the ones making the sounds and not something naturally occurring like water dripping.

There are the two basic types of haunts we see most often. An intelligent haunt is a spirit that can see, hear, acknowledge, or interact with us. They answer our questions and generally function the same as those of us who are living. These spirits are the ones we are trying to help. A residual haunt refers to a release of energy that we witness in the right place or the right time. The first experience

I had in Gettysburg is an extreme example of this. Think of it as a piece of film being played out in front of you: you can see a ghost walking across a room and call out to them, but they don't notice you at all. It could happen once or it could happen every day at the same exact time. By asking questions in this space, we were verifying that this haunting was intelligent.

"Okay," I asked, "can you knock on the count of three? One."

I paused and waited. If a knock were to happen then, maybe it was something we could debunk. It was quiet.

"Two." We waited. Were they listening? I like to push my luck during these situations. I wanted to test if the spirit was truly in control of the conversation.

"Two and a half." Amy had a tiny smirk on her face. I think she was anticipating the count of three just as much as the spirits were.

"Three," I said finally. A moment, a breath, a beat. Then, a knock.

"It was right there! Right there!" My heart felt like it was going to pound out of my chest. Neither of us could believe it. Sometimes when Amy and I have really intense experiences, we have the weirdest reactions, laughing and giggling like kids. I know that doesn't seem like an appropriate reaction, especially thinking about it from the spirit's perspective. We apologized to the nurses, but we couldn't help ourselves. Finding evidence of the paranormal might be our jobs, but that excitement of discovery never goes away. Hearing a knock coming from the darkness of a haunted, abandoned sanatorium in the middle of the night—on command no less—was so strange and surreal that we had to laugh. Not because it was funny, but because it added to our theory that when you humanize spirits and treat them as equals, you get strong activity in response.

"I'm sorry," Amy said, composing herself. "We don't mean to laugh."

There was silence. We wanted to make sure that whomever we were speaking with knew that our reaction was because of the results, not them personally. But maybe we had unintentionally offended them—or maybe they were just waiting and listening. Moving the conversation along and trying to gauge this new dynamic, I placed my hand on the frame of the nearest window and said, "If you are knocking for us, please, would you mind knocking right next to my hand?"

Sure enough, a knock happened right where I asked for it to be. I could feel the vibration. Whoever was there with us was still invested and hadn't lost interest. This had moved beyond any doubt—we were connecting with a spirit, or multiple spirits, and they wanted to communicate. Paranormal TV shows might make it seem like this kind of thing happens all the time, but in reality, it's incredibly rare.

Amy and I had never experienced anything like it. We needed to move away from commanded actions if we wanted to try and figure out who they were. If there was any chance to get to know them, this was the only opportunity. We asked the spirits to knock once for a "yes" answer and knock twice for "no." Our series of questions confirmed that they were nurses, and that they felt stuck in that location. We asked them if they felt as though they were being taken advantage of, and they communicated that they didn't mind people coming into their space and interacting with them.

"How many of you are in this space?" I asked. "If each of you, one at a time, could knock wherever you are, we will be able to count."

The first knock was to my right, and then another a little further down to the left. Then another and another. Some were stronger knocks and others were gentle taps. In the end, we counted about thirteen to fourteen nurses in the space. It felt like this was supposed to be happening: we were connecting to people who were no longer living, in a space that had been newly opened just for us. This was their chance for…something…but what? Amy and I both were at a loss. How could we help them? What could we do for them?

At this stage in our investigation, Amy and I had already had a life-changing experience. The interaction alone was enough to keep us fueled for years to come, but it wasn't just about us. We felt instinctively that to leave at this point without giving anything in return would render meaningless any experience we'd had. We wanted communication, but these spirits *needed* something. Imagine being a spirit—having all the human traits, wants, and needs as you did when you were alive—but now you exist in some other form where it's hard, if not impossible, for anyone to hear you or see you. When you need something, you can't get it for yourself and you must rely on the living to provide it for you, which is especially challenging when opportunities to communicate are few. What if you never come into contact with a paranormal investigator, or anyone who's actually looking for you? The nurses were in a place that was routinely investigated, but in a part of the hospital where people couldn't go. This was their first chance in a long time to make contact, and it seemed like they were eager to get their message heard.

The one thing we could offer them was prayer. In that moment, we felt that a word of prayer was the one thing that we could do that might give them some sort of comfort or peace.

"Do you want us to pray for you?" Amy asked. One solid, clear knock reverberated through the long dark hallway.

We had found through past investigations that the idea and act of prayer can ease the activity in some locations. We use "God" as a universal term, since we can't assume what religion they followed.

In this instance, we offered a non-denominational prayer of comfort, peace, and remembrance.

"Dear God," I began, "we would like to pray for those who are trapped here. If you could just comfort them and help them to be free again…and tell them that we care very deeply about them. In your name we do pray. Amen."

Silence, once more, enveloped us. We could feel a slight shift in the air. There weren't any knocks while we said our prayer. They were concentrating and observing. They took in what we had to say and gave us the chance to try and do something for them. A few moments after, knocks began again, not far away as they had been, but all around us…as if to say thank you for what we just did.

Amy and I were emotionally spent at this point. We had the incredible high of this experience, but now were experiencing the deepest low of not being able to do more for them. The feeling of sadness and helplessness was compounded by our physical exhaustion. This experience had been going on for quite some time at that point. Our crew was about to go into overtime because it was so late, and we had no choice but to leave. We had never been at such a loss before. I wrapped my arm around Amy's shoulder and we made the long, slow walk back to the entrance. As we left, the knocks followed one by one as if to say, "Come back, don't leave. Please don't go."

We wanted to do something more, but at the time we couldn't. The production schedule wasn't dictated by us, and we weren't permitted the time to go back. But the experience fundamentally changed us. The path of investigation that we had been on for so long was developing into a less self-serving act. We started giving more of our attention to the needs of spirits, rather than focusing on getting reactions from spirits for our own purposes. Our goal was shifting towards the idea that we could make a connection with ghosts to better understand what they wanted or needed, to try and help them because they couldn't do it for themselves. What was so painful about our experience with the nurses is that we could tell they needed something from us, something more than we were able to give them that night, and that we had to walk away without being able to figure out what that was.

Amy and I have been back to Waverly Hills since, but we haven't made contact with those nurses again. We went back to film an episode of *Kindred Spirits* and arrived at the sanatorium with every intention of going to the nurses' wing and reconnecting with those spirits. But when we got there, owner Tina Mattingly told us that she had been experiencing aggressive activity that scared her. We immediately knew that we would have to focus our investigation on the area and the phenomena that Tina needed us to. Not only does she own the property, but she also lives there, so she's pretty brave when it comes to the supernatural; if she had an experience that was terrifying and unexplainable to her, then it was very serious. We would have to wait to make contact with the nurses until next time.

Amy and I knew definitively that we wanted more from what we were doing in the paranormal. We had spent many years providing peace to the living by giving them answers, whether it was confirming that they really were experiencing something paranormal or debunking the activity. They wanted answers and we provided them.

It became clearer and clearer that we had an opportunity to do more, to try and give spirits all the same answers we were giving living clients. But we couldn't accomplish that goal in our present situation. There came a point where we felt like it was time to leave *Ghost Hunters*.

Believe it or not, that was more than two years after our Waverly experience. During that time, we tried to do our best to incorporate more human compassion into our methods. We started to notice we would have incredible activity because of how we approached with open hearts and minds, but we were not in charge of our own investigations and we were at the mercy of someone else's schedule. We didn't have the time and space we needed to do the kind of investigating we wanted, and no amount of asking would change that.

In 2012, things changed for us both. After Amy had her daughter in October, she didn't want to be on the road all the time because she had a newborn. I had gotten married in August, and my husband and I started a non-profit theater company in Provincetown. We were focusing on building a future, which was very hard to do while on the road eight months out of the year.

Amy and I continued to be on the road for another solid year. We tried to make it work because we loved the people we worked with and we had hope that those we worked for would see what kind of sacrifice we were all making. One day toward the beginning of 2014, when our current contracts were coming to a close and we were about to wrap another season, Amy said to me, "I just don't think I can keep doing this. I am not sure if I am going to sign on for another season."

We discussed this for several days on our very last case we filmed. I felt the same way she did. We were exhausted by what we were currently doing, and we wanted more. "Well," I said, "if you aren't going to be here, I sure as hell don't want to be here."

After the third or fourth inquiry from people at networks who had heard we had left *Ghost Hunters*, Amy and I sat down and drafted our ideas for a documentary-style paranormal investigation show. Ben came up with the title, *Kindred Spirits*. What was written on that paper is exactly what you see today streaming directly into your homes. Our idea was to not only go into a location and have experiences, but to find out the who, what, and why of the haunt. Most importantly, above anything else, we wanted to help the living *and* the dead. We use research to inform and enhance our investigations, trying to answer the greatest question of all, "Why do the dead linger and what can we learn from it?"

CHAPTER 5

Reconciling Religion and the Afterlife

Growing up in Muscle Shoals, Alabama, church was a big part of my childhood. My parents weren't that religious, but every Sunday, Grannie would make sure my brother and I were sitting in a pew at Central Baptist Church. As a child I was "saved" and baptized in the same baptismal tank as my family—but the more sure I became of who I was as a person, the harder it was to feel any connection to a church where the pastor found any excuse to preach against the "evils" of homosexuality. As I got older and found peace within myself, I became more and more estranged from a church that was sermonizing about AIDS as God's punishment for gay men and that the entire LGBTQ+ community was going to suffer eternal damnation.

By the time I reached high school, I had broken away from traditional organized religion. I had to do it in order to survive, but that doesn't mean that I am not spiritual or that I don't believe in God. Nowadays, I have complicated feelings about what heaven and hell are, not just whether they really exist, but whether they are different for people depending on their beliefs. But also, I think my connection to a higher power is deeper because now I am doing it on my own terms. I make no excuses for who I am as a person and God continues to truly bless my life with so many wonderful things.

The study and practice of understanding paranormal phenomena is in and of itself a kind of belief system. Religious practice is grounded completely in belief and faith, and so is the exploration of supernatural phenomena. While we don't belong to a single organization or possess a unified idea of God in the paranormal community—for example, many people who question the existence of a higher power believe in ghosts and metaphysical concepts—the underlying philosophy is the same. Those of us who take what we do very seriously often study texts about the paranormal, which lead us to have our own theories as to why ghostly activity occurs and how to communicate with spirits. Also, we seek to learn from those who have scholarly ideas about the spiritual world. The one thing we all have in common is faith that there is more going on around us than meets the eye.

None of us can really know, without a doubt, what's after this life until we get there. Or can we? The more time I have spent researching the paranormal in my life, the more sure I've become that communicating with ghosts on this plane of existence can teach me about the afterlife. I believe it's possible to find out more about what happens after we die from ghosts that we encounter during paranormal investigations. They can teach us about what it's like wherever they are, and can help shed some light on why some ghosts stay behind. If there really is someplace else for spirits to go after they die, why haven't the ghosts who have stayed behind made the ultimate transition to where they are supposed to be?

For me, the obvious answer is that if a spirit is doomed to face hell for eternity—or, putting aside whether that's actually true, if a person who has died *believes* they will go to hell if they move on—I can absolutely see why they might want to hang on to this earthly realm a bit longer. I mean, if you get to make the decision after you die, the choice seems pretty clear between eternal damnation or hanging out behind the veil with a bunch of mortals.

Why not ask the source, you might wonder. As paranormal investigators, we have access to non-living people who, as far as we can surmise, have experience with the other side. Surely a ghost or two will be able to inform us of what is actually going on, right? Not so fast.

Talking to Spirits About the Great Beyond

In fact, most of the contact we have with spirits is void of the topics of heaven and hell, or any serious questioning about what the afterlife is like. It really never comes up in conversation. Usually, we are focused on trying to find out what they need or want. Whether the spirit knows anything about their version of heaven is not important in terms of what we are trying to accomplish, and holds very little weight.

However, on occasion, we have asked. When Amy and I have brought it up, it's usually because we know something about a ghost's spiritual beliefs in life—specifically, when we find out that the person we are trying to contact in spirit form was not religious or didn't believe in ghosts or anything paranormal in life. That situation raises such interesting questions. Now that they're in spirit communicating with us, have their views and thoughts changed?

Have they learned anything about the hereafter? What about ghosts? Do they believe in themselves?

There was a case from season six of *Kindred Spirits* where we were in Newburgh, New York, investigating a home where an older woman, Ray, and her adult daughter, LeAnne, were experiencing strong activity. It was so intense that Ray was sleeping during the day and staying up all night because what she heard and saw was so disquieting. She and her ex-husband had experienced something truly eerie: they both had heart attacks on the same day. She recovered, but he didn't—and after her near-death state, she reported waking up from her coma in the hospital and feeling someone patting her on the thigh saying, "It's okay, it's okay, it's okay." She noticed the strong smell of Old Spice and realized it was her ex-husband, Richard. She didn't yet know he had died that day. At the time, they were living apart and their communication with each other was sparse.

A few weeks later, as she lay in bed trying to sleep, Ray recalled seeing a big bright light over her bedroom mirror and hearing familiar voices coming from this light. They were saying, "Go away, go away, not yet, it's not your time." She said she was reliving what happened during her recent near-death heart attack experience. We'll get more into near-death experiences later, but isn't that the most incredible story you've ever heard? Heart attacks *on the same day*, and her husband telling her to walk away from the light and go back to her body? It still blows my mind.

She had a strong feeling it might be her ex-husband haunting the house, so Amy and I used the information we knew about him to assist in our investigation. One of the things we knew for sure was that he wasn't the least bit religious. His connection to any sort of higher power grew even more distant after the death of their three-year-old child many years back. The man didn't believe in an afterlife when he was alive, yet there he was as a ghost, in a house his ex-wife was currently living in.

It didn't make it into the final cut of the episode, but I really wanted to lean into this contradiction of a ghost not believing in an afterlife (at least, when he was living). When I bring up anything religious on a case it comes from a positive and well-meaning place, but it does have its roots in things I was taught as a child. Sometimes, I bring up religious topics that I don't follow anymore.

Once we were set up in the house, I asked Ray's ex-husband a straightforward question: "Do you believe in heaven?"

The response we got back was an intense "YES."

"If you now believe in heaven," I continued, "why aren't you there?" I wanted to know if he wasn't allowed in because of his lack of faith, or whether he was choosing to stay behind.

He didn't say anything else about it.

I was hoping to find out more information, but we didn't get any other answers to explain why this person, who was non-living and didn't believe in any religion when he was alive, now believed that heaven existed. That was truly frustrating. If he were to just speak up and tell us what he knew, or at least explain why he now felt that way, it could comfort a lot of people searching for those answers. Maybe by staying behind, he was trying to do more and connect with the living for a purpose, to gain some sort of redemption before the final judgment. Whatever the reason, his being around led to more questions than answers. He didn't ask for prayer, and we got the impression he didn't want it.

Other spirits are the exact opposite. The nurses in the wing at Waverly Hills wanted prayer, and we knew, deep down, that they needed it, whether it was just for their comfort and peace of mind, or whether it helped them get somewhere they wanted to go.

There was a case that Amy and I did in season two of *Kindred Spirits* in Corning, New York, where a man was experiencing activity so strong that he wasn't using the upstairs of his house, where his bedroom was located, and instead was sleeping on the couch in his living room.

The house had notable history because the inventor of the electric chair once occupied the property; the owner thought maybe the spirit of that man was causing him this uneasiness and turmoil. He was so preoccupied with the activity that he was distracted and fearful all the time. The haunt had taken over his life. He tried his best to get rid of the problem by asking his friends over to investigate for him. They were fairly new to paranormal explorations and their methods were a bit harsh. They communicated with an aggressive and accusatory tone that wasn't necessarily wrong, but wasn't the most conducive to getting informational responses to questions.

We spent days trying to unravel this mystery, but the spirit in the upstairs part of the house was so frightened that they would not communicate with us, and trying to get responses became much more difficult as the days went on. It wasn't until we began to discuss the lives of the former owners of the property that we made any progress. We were able to spark interest and gain trust by recalling moments in their past that they would enjoy speaking about. We knew the elderly woman who had lived in the home previously was a devout Christian who was very attached to her church. When we brought that up, we finally got responses. It turned out that the spirit was of that sweet older lady, who had passed away some years before. She was misidentified and, up to that point, wasn't given the proper respect she deserved. As we spoke to her, we realized that she didn't know why she was still in her home. It seemed like she was frightened, lonely, and most certainly wanted to leave.

"Do you have a reason to be here?" I asked in an EVP session.

"I don't know," she responded on the recording.

"Would you like to leave?" I asked.

The answer was a forceful, emphatic, "YES!"

When she started giving us answers, I immediately lost it. I was emotional, tears streaming down my face. I had lost my grannie at this point, and I imagined what it would be like if this lady were her. It broke me.

We offered her prayer as a way to bring her peace on the other side, but it was healing for us as well. We needed a reset. Prayer, as a private meditative act, worked for us as a focused spiritual dialogue that helped us process a difficult situation.

Can Ghosts Come and Go—or Be Summoned Back— from Another Place?

There are countless people living today who don't participate in paranormal investigations or may not strongly believe in ghosts. Yet, they believe a deceased friend or family member has made their presence known after they have passed. They aren't experiencing a haunting but rather a "visit." We've explored the idea that some spirits are already in a peaceful afterlife somewhere, and occasionally they join us here on earth for a short time. On some investigations, a familial spirit pops in and communicates with us, but isn't the dominant entity in the space. They aren't the focus of our investigation or the cause of the worrisome activity but they needed to reach out and say something. This usually provides comfort for our clients, most of whom believe that the activity in their home is being caused by a departed relative, when in actuality it is not.

Most of the time, the spirits causing the main activity have no connection to the current occupants. However, we've seen instances where a deceased family member will pop in just for a moment and say a few words of encouragement that we can pass on, and then they are never heard from again while we are investigating. To me, it's as if those departed souls were called to us in that situation.

Maybe our collective living energy and the hope or want from the client triggers this relative to show up. I love to think of it in that way because it seems to be the most positive and comforting idea. Not only do you get to experience an afterlife, but you are sometimes whisked away to the realm of the living to make a connection when a person you love needs you.

As much as I believe it's possible for someone to come back by choice, I also believe the living can call on those who have passed to join us, even if they are not related to one another, especially in an investigation or séance. The power of the living is strong, and I think with strong intention and manifestation we can ask those who have passed to join us and speak with us.

The act of connecting to or conjuring the dead has spanned thousands of years. Some of our current techniques have been developed and passed down through generations of spiritualists, mediums, and paranormal investigators. On a case not so long ago, Amy and I went back to the very roots of our practice.

We were investigating an old hotel in the historic market district of Palmyra, New York. The building was part of a collection of preserved old buildings in town, and had been moved to its current location. Previously in that spot, a home had burned in a horrible fire; the lives of a mother and her six children were lost.

Two years prior to our arrival, there had been another fire across the street at the laundromat. Ever since then, the activity in the area had increased. This hotel building was *extremely* haunted. In fact, the entire block had activity in every building; since the local historical society owned all of it, we had access to the entire paranormal district.

We wanted to try a technique we had utilized in the past, where we gather information from other ghosts in the area. It might be that they had noticed something different at the place we were currently investigating. Though we were there because activity had ramped up recently, we got the impression that most of the spirits in the market district were living their best ghostly lives. They were free to move around the area and were in communication with other entities.

Amy and I headed three buildings down from the hotel where a lovely spirit, Sybil Phelps, was said to have resided. Sybil had lived during the heyday of the modern spiritualist movement, a system of belief or religious practice based on communication with the spirits of the dead, especially through mediums. Palmyra is close to where spiritualism started, in Hydesville, New York.

She had been very involved in her spiritualist community and even spearheaded the historic preservation of the Fox sisters' home, who claimed to have open communication through knocking with a man they called Mr. Splitfoot. The Fox sisters made their original claims in 1848, and inspired a whole movement of people attempting to communicate with the other side and find closure from their losses, especially during the Civil War.

Spiritualism was Sybil's religion, her belief system. We wanted to connect with her and ask if she noticed the fire at the laundromat or any other changes on the block, especially at the hotel. We invited our friend and psychic medium Heather Rease Mattison to join us for this experiment, because we were going to perform a classic séance and conjure the spirit of Sybil to the table.

For the séance, we had some of her original spiritualist tools: her personal séance table, her metaphysical books we could use as trigger objects, her original crystal ball, and a picture of Sybil in a beautiful gold frame. We sat in her parlor, where she had held many of these same rituals; we lit candles around the room, dimmed the lights, placed her photograph at the head of the table, and prepared to make contact. We all held hands, took a deep breath, and called out to her.

"Sybil, if you can hear us, if you're in the house, we've saved a place for you," I said. "We travel the country and the world looking for the non-living, those that are like you."

We heard footsteps from the room directly across from us, in the dining room.

"If you are here, can you please say your name for us?" Amy asked. "We have a question we think only you can help us with. There was a fire next door and many lives were lost. And then there was another fire across the street from here that happened more recently. They're saying that the energy and the spirits in that house next door are more active than they used to be. Do you interact with anyone connected to that house and property who might have died there?"

Sure enough, she spoke to us through our recorder. She said her name, she knew what we were doing, and she also confirmed for us that she didn't notice any change or new activity surrounding the fire that happened at the laundromat. This was so incredible on multiple levels. She answered our questions for the investigation, but for me, the most important takeaway was that we had made contact with someone whose religion had revolved around the idea that we could communicate with the dead. Amy and I had the rare opportunity to connect with someone who was one of our paranormal forebears. What she believed in when she was alive is the basis of what we do now.

When Sybil was alive, she believed that the living could contact the non-living and now she was able to prove it once again even in a ghostly form. We called her to us through methods she believed in, and were able to conjure her spirit. She sat at the table with us. It was a vindication of her life's work to be conjured after her death using her own methodology.

When Religion and Study of the Paranormal Intersect

Paranormal researcher Greg Newkirk was raised Baptist, the son and grandson of ministers. He and his wife Dana Newkirk are paranormal investigators, researchers, and documentarians who have been on *Kindred Spirits* many times.

"I think that people who have genuinely curious minds begin to question the things that they are given, instead of the things that they have discovered," he said to me recently. "As a kid who grew up with a dad who was a fairly strict practicing Baptist minister, I was supposed to be a Baptist minister. I was supposed to take up the family line. It was a traumatic experience for everyone when I started asking questions. Those questions started early and they started with the idea of 'What about aliens on another planet? Have they heard about Jesus? What are they going to do? Are they going to have to go to hell because they haven't heard about Jesus?' Then I found *Coast to Coast AM* with Art Bell, I found *Unsolved Mysteries*, I found *The X-Files*. Like most kids do, I started to have an interest in the things that my parents told me I shouldn't read about or listen to. When they said things like, 'That's a trick—the devil's trying to trick you,' it only made me more curious."

The first time he tried to go ghost hunting (but wasn't allowed to) was when Greg felt a real break with the religion he was raised in. "I asked why, and the questions spiraled," he said. "I was twelve years old. My friends and I didn't know what we were doing. We were just reading books by Hans Holzer and Ed and Lorraine Warren." The Warrens, who investigated the house from *The Conjuring* and the Annabelle doll, had a religious component to their work.

"I tried to use that to justify paranormal investigation to my parents," he said. "Like, 'Look, you can be religious and you can do this from a religious perspective.' But that only scared them more."

Being frightened of the unknown is only natural. What you do with those feelings is the thing that counts. I think it's important to ask bigger questions and explore larger fundamental ideas, beyond what we're taught. For me, and many others, the paranormal is that avenue to understanding.

When it comes to grasping the concept of the afterlife, both religion and ghost exploration are heavily focused on the end-of-life transition, whether that's to another state of being or to a heavenly plane.

"I think that as long as there are religious people investigating the paranormal, there's no way to take it out. The way that they see the afterlife is colored by their religious beliefs," Greg said. "I also know that the paranormal is a thing that you need to experience subjectively, and that involves your religious beliefs or lack thereof. I would not call myself religious anymore. I would call myself spiritual. I think that the difference a lot of the time between religion and spirituality is that religion is looking outward for something as opposed to spirituality, which is an inward search."

I believe that spirituality plays a greater role in communication with spirits than religion does. Finding answers and reconciling fears about our own mortality can only be achieved by exploring that inner layer of our core beliefs, asking questions, and trying to process those answers. Paranormal investigation takes that one step further by exploring the idea of communicating with those who've passed on, and having faith that it can be achieved. If all our family and friends who have died are somewhere up among the stars, we try to answer the question: *How can we gain a direct line of communication with them?*

I think it is important to explore the difference between religion and spirituality in paranormal investigation. Religion has a specific structure—as Greg said, an outward expression—while using one's own spiritual beliefs is somewhat free flowing. I think connecting to the afterlife, grounded in your own spiritual presence, is the best way to communicate with those that have moved on.

"Spirituality," Greg said, "is very important when it comes to having a genuine encounter that is not colored by how somebody else has painted it, but by how we need to see it."

"For me, I think spirituality is an intuitive process," Dana added. "It's that intuition that exists within us, and because it's personal, it can take whatever road it needs to, there's no restriction. Whereas with religion, we are contained, we have rules, we have prescribed ways of doing things. It's fine if that's what works for you, but I think spirituality is that kind of intuitive current that we can travel and jump around on. When it comes to paranormal research and paranormal things in general, I think an element of spirituality is really beneficial for most people. It could be spirituality as a higher concept, like the afterlife or God, but often it's more so that intuitive kind of feeling within ourselves.

"It gives you access to your own intuition without judgment," she continued. "I think it's really beneficial for most people to reach into those spaces. For me, it's always been an intuitive thing, and it's always felt hand in hand with paranormal investigation. I kind of came into both of those two things at the very same time. So it made sense to me, as a teenager, and over the years, that spirituality and paranormal research mesh very well together. I think it has to do with that intuitive exploration."

Can We Use Religion to Make a Deeper Connection with the Spirit World?

This is an enormous question, but I can only tackle this question from the ideas I have been taught. I have explored many other religions, and there is common ground between various belief systems, but I can only dissect the paranormal and religion through the lens that I know. It's very important to acknowledge, though, that there are many different religions, and especially in paranormal study in the Western world, Christianity has largely overtaken them.

"I think you have one religion that is dictating the entire experience for everyone, which is kind of the case right now," Dana said. "We have the initial founders of this paranormal community, people like the Warrens and Holzer, who are really bringing in heavy Christian overtones and dictating the way that people experience it. You can talk to someone who's a paranormal investigator who maybe has never set foot in a church in their entire life, but they wholeheartedly believe in demonic possession. It pushes out other religious beliefs and perspectives."

When learning about the paranormal, it's important to keep that in your mind: that most of the English language information out there, especially the books held up as seminal texts on the supernatural, are coming from a deeply Western, Christian perspective. "I think that's when it becomes problematic," she added. "It's when you have this kind of blanket idea of what paranormal investigation is and it's really been dictated to the community by overtly Western religious beliefs. I have so many friends who are Muslim, Pagan, and other non-Christian religions, and they have their own very distinct ideas of what paranormal research is like. When you talk to people with different religious faiths, it can enhance your own ideas. It's a better thing when you have a prism of that kind shining light on something, versus a single perspective."

Almost every major organized religion acknowledges the paranormal in its own way. In Hinduism, the world's oldest religion, families observe yearlong mourning rituals so that their departed family members won't become *preta*, or hungry ghosts, who are excluded from the cycle of reincarnation and who remain in a suspended state. Buddhists and Taoists in China and other East Asian countries observe Ghost Month, a ritual going back two millennia. During Ghost Month, the Hungry Ghost Festival both honors ancestors and involves rituals to ward off wandering spirits who may be looking to cause harm.

Islam is the world's second most prevalent religion (24 percent of the world population, according to Pew Research). In that faith, jinn are unseen spirits who have a parallel existence to humans, and aren't necessarily what we think of as ghosts. "They see us, but we cannot see them. In very rare cases humans and jinn can interact with each other," said Shaykh Waleed Basyouni, Ph.D., President of AlMaghrib Institute and head of its Islamic Theology and Ethics Department. "Allah created them to have their own life. They don't bother themselves by our existence. They live and share with us the earth, but they have their own system, their own life, and we have our life as well."

Those jinn can even create what I would interpret as activity caused by ghosts, if I were experiencing it myself. "We know of jinn who live in houses," Basyouni said. "So many times, in your house, you might hear something or you feel something walking or a presence of a certain energy around you, but you don't see it. This will be the jinn. For us as Muslim, we know that this is normal. Basically, you live your life. They're not supposed to harm you. They're not supposed to bother you. They have their life and I have my life."

While Christianity is my religious foundation, as we move forward in this chapter, I encourage people to go out and seek answers from many different sources. We can learn from each other and our differences. For instance, Dana is a practicing hedgewitch from whom I have gained a lot of insight into magick rituals in belief, investigation, and daily life. (Magick, spelled with a "k," rather than ending with a "c," relates to the practice of actual magic through Wicca, neopaganism, or modern witchcraft, instead of an illusion or stage magic.)

The Theological Foundation of Ghost Hunting

From what I have observed, the Christian Bible is the ammunition religious people most often use to dismiss supernatural theories. Some people love to use scripture as a weapon rather than a tool. I feel like I've heard it all: that being Wiccan or Pagan is the practice of those who are connected to hell; and tarot cards, psychics and divination, and ritual magick are all tools of dark arts. And God forbid you dare to mention Ouija boards—their heads might just explode.

It never crossed my mind that being interested in the paranormal could be perceived as a bad thing until someone said it to me as an adult. I was always capable of believing in what I wanted and creating my own spiritual sanctuary. Once I had a platform to talk about the paranormal, the critics came flooding in, many sending me messages of doom or telling me I was sinning against God. I have received countless emails, messages, and comments on social media, saying that we are promoting devilish ideas and that every spirit we encounter is a demon. Some people quote scripture to me and get offended if I express different views about the situation.

But through my research, I have found surprising commonalities between what's in the Bible and metaphysical ideas on the afterlife. That overlap changed the way I saw what I do as a paranormal researcher. Even though I knew what I was doing wasn't taboo, because so many critics used scripture to "prove" I was doing something wrong, there always used to be a little doubt in the back of my mind that maybe they were right. After my own research into new ideas on biblical text, those doubts have quickly faded away.

The Bible discusses many topics that are metaphysical in nature. The holy ghost or holy spirit, by definition, is God in the form of a spirit. Believers claim to feel him all around, to sense his power, to witness things brought on by the spirit, or to be overcome with the holy ghost. Also in the text, there are angels, demons, visitations by the dead, crisis apparitions (those that appear when they are at the brink of their own death or having just passed away), and other manifestations that seem supernatural in nature. People have prophetic visions, while others seek out psychics for help in connecting with the dead. Even today, preachers and religious leaders say they have dreams in which God tells them what to do, or in which they see something they want to warn their congregation about.

I've encountered spirits and ghosts, felt their presence, witnessed them in full view, and been overcome by their energy or power. I know that psychics can connect to those on the other side, and sometimes share predictions of future events. These things, to me, are beyond dispute. Yet traditional Christian views denounce all of those things.

I wanted to better understand specific biblical texts that include what we could classify as paranormal phenomena, so I spoke to Matt Arnold, a Christian researcher and writer from the United Kingdom who has a Masters in Pioneering Ministries from Manchester University. Matt is also very interested in the paranormal, and has used theology in his investigation. He aims to educate other Christians on biblical text and meaning as a means to better understand our supernatural world.

"I ended up doing a couple of papers on ministry amongst Pagans during my Masters study, and my thesis was on paranormal hauntings and deliverance applications, and that changed me completely," he told me.

"So, what you can try to do is to say, 'Yeah, we respect the scriptures highly, and because we respect the scriptures so highly, we want to know what was in the mind of the original writer when they penned those particular words at that time in the development of the Hebraic faith,'" Matt explained. "What did it mean at that moment in time? Because it evolves over time. When you get to about 300 BC, you end up with writers going, 'Well, we need to speak about an afterlife that is unseen. We'll use the word Hades because Hades, *Awides*, means unseen.' So, the words that they were using had meanings specifically, and they intended those meanings to be understood by their readers, because the Bible wasn't written with 21st century people in mind. So obviously it uses the language, the cultural imagery, and the theological understanding that existed at that moment in time."

It stands to reason that the way we think about ghosts today isn't necessarily the same as how people a thousand years ago thought about them. "Ghosts are mentioned in different words in the Bible," Matt said. He pointed to 1 Samuel 28, which touches on the idea of an "Ob," which Matt defined as an ancestral spirit.

In the story, Saul had cast out all the mediums, psychics, and soothsayers from the land. On the brink of war, he asks the Lord what to do because he is afraid. However, Saul was no longer receiving any messages from God by dreams, Urim (lights or fire), or prophets. Not getting the guidance he is looking for, Saul makes his servants seek out a woman, referred to as a "ghost mistress," who is a medium. He disguises himself and goes to this psychic, asking her to conjure up his friend Samuel, a ruler now passed, so that he can seek guidance. Lo and behold she does, and channels a very specific message from Samuel, who is referred to as an Ob in the text because he is called forth from the great beyond. And the message was...not good. Essentially, the ghost of Samuel says, Saul didn't do God's will, so God has abandoned him and soon Saul and his sons will join him on the other side. Saul and his sons were killed in battle the next day. In this one story, we have a psychic medium, the conjuring of a ghost, and an intense prophetic message.

The recognition and documentation of paranormal phenomena in biblical text proves that what I study has been taken seriously for thousands of years. The language of the text and the scripture doesn't give us any impression, at least from God, that the ghost mistress was doing anything wrong. The entire story is matter of fact. Saul, who banished all the psychics from the kingdom, cast the first stone and hypocritically sought comfort in the very thing he was against. Doesn't get more *Game of Thrones* than that.

People commonly cite Hebrews 9:27 as scriptural evidence that ghosts don't exist, but Matt believes that interpretation comes from a too-narrow reading of the text. The passage reads, "And just as it is appointed for man to die once, and after that comes judgment, so Christ, having been offered once to bear the sins of many, will appear a second time, not to deal with sin, but to save those who are eagerly waiting for him."

"People always start with, 'it is appointed for,' and it doesn't begin that way, it's 'And just as,'" Matt explained. "There's a comparison between 'it is appointed for a man to die once' and 'after that comes judgment.' This is a statement comparing the period between the crucifixion and second coming, and between a person dying and facing judgment. Just as there is at least a 2,023-year gap between Jesus dying and his second coming, it can be argued that there is a time lapse between a person dying and the judgment.

Rather than being an argument against the existence of ghosts, the sentence in its entirety actually opens up the possibility of an intermediate state for those who have died."

To me, it's an even stronger argument once you layer in the idea of ghosts staying behind because of unfinished business. It might be that they have work to do in the afterlife before the final judgment. Could that be what Catholicism talks about as purgatory, the suspended place that's neither heaven nor hell? That theory could explain ghosts who are essentially still trying to live their lives, staying in their homes and sometimes being angry about new owners making changes to their space—they're in a suspended state before they get to the next life.

That idea could also explain why we think some spirits come and go, as if they aren't always here, but reappear when we need or when they need to communicate something. Maybe they are working in the afterlife, trying to do some good, to help make positive impacts and continue their own spiritual journey. On the other hand, maybe those spirits who are aggressive in their actions were jerks in life so they continue to be jerks when they are dead. They have time on their hands. Their own self-interests take precedence over any good they could be doing. So, it takes a paranormal investigation to speak with them about why they are acting out and to try and help them. When they realize there may be a better way of going about their current existence, the activity subsides.

Our conversation was eye-opening to me because I had never considered how the scripture of my youth could intersect with my beliefs about the paranormal as an adult. Matt's ideas have made me consider different options when making a connection with those spirits we are trying to help.

My biggest question, though, was whether Jesus himself had anything to say about ghosts. "Twice Jesus could have informed us that ghosts do not exist," Matt said. He *could* have said that, but he didn't. The first instance is in Matthew 14:22–33, when the disciples see Jesus walking on the water and think he's a ghost, and again in Luke 24:36–43, when Jesus appears to the disciples and says that he is not a ghost.

"On neither occasion does he take the opportunity to challenge the cultural beliefs the disciples had regarding ghosts as spirits of the dead," he added. The important distinction is that Jesus indicates, 'I'm not a ghost,' not 'Ghosts aren't real.'

"The irony of the Jesus walking on water story is that in Greco-Roman ghost stories, ghosts don't walk on water," Matt explained. "Only divine beings walk on water. So, what was being telegraphed by Jesus there is 'Hello guys, I'm a divine being.' The disciples are going, 'Nah. No, don't be stupid. It's got to be a ghost. Yeah. Jesus can't be a divine being. He's got to be a ghost.' But then ghosts don't walk on water."

There you have it: discussion of ghosts, and calling them forth from the great beyond, in the text most often cited as evidence that ghosts aren't real, or that ghosts are really demons trying to do the devil's bidding. I don't want to get into the demonic debate here, but let me just say, people too easily conflate ghosts and demons, and there are those who throw that word around recklessly. In my experience, the paranormal activity I've witnessed has almost never, ever been even remotely connected to anything demonic— which is a serious, and totally separate, issue. You might have a ghost knocking on your wall, but unless you are one of a tiny handful of unfortunate souls, you are almost definitely not in contact with a demon.

It's an easy leap, though, and I understand why so many people talk about ghosts and demons interchangeably. It boils down to simple fear of something unexplained happening around you.

You're sensing something is happening, and it's easy to assume that strange, scary thing is actually an evil thing. (Thanks, horror movies!) The simplest way I can put it is this: ghosts are people, they're just people who exist in a different state of awareness. They're not trying to hurt you and they're certainly not capable of possessing you or stealing your soul.

Using Religious Tools in Paranormal Investigation

When a spirit asks for prayer and I know what religion this person practiced in life—if it falls in line with what I know—then I can pray for them in a way that would make sense to them, using words that would be familiar to them. If they ask for prayer and I have no idea what religion they are, I usually offer up a prayer that speaks to God, love, light, and peace, to try to be as broad and comforting as possible. The idea of God can cover any number of beliefs.

In these instances, I am hoping that the energy and sentiment I am giving out comes across as sincere and as truthful as possible. I think spirits can feel what kind of vibe we are giving off more than anyone knows. Like, you can't be in a bad mood and successfully look for ghosts. They don't want to be around that negativity, just like living people don't. So, a truthful and heartfelt statement or prayer will work if the spirit is accepting of it, and as long as what you're offering isn't just lip service. When we've used prayer in investigations, it's always a powerful moment because it's something that allows the deceased person to feel some sort of peace in their world.

There was a case on *Ghost Hunters* where we visited the Old City Jail in Charleston, South Carolina. The claims in this location included shadow figures, disembodied sounds, and voices; there was an entity in the building that made some people very afraid, and would attack some that were on tours. This place had also functioned as a poor house: if a husband was in jail and his family had no way to support themselves, his wife and children would also be locked up. It was a very sad, oppressive place.

Late in the evening, we went in to investigate. While we were asking our normal questions, one of our producers said she felt something burning on her waist line. We looked, and she had scratches from hip to hip. We ran through all the protocol: did she bump into something, was she having an allergic reaction, etc. None of those things came into play. We continued our investigation, and not five minutes later she was attacked again, this time on the neck. She had four scratches. Then more appeared on her back.

At this point, she was very afraid and didn't want to be in the building anymore. I told her that it was a scary thing, but that she couldn't leave. "If you leave they win," I said. She knew what I meant. Sometimes you have to face your fears, especially with those in the spirit realm who may try to harm you, in order to show them that the living have more power over the dead. "Hold your ground and don't take any crap" has always been my motto in this kind of situation.

While I firmly believe that most spirits aren't trying to hurt you, people commonly get scratched by them. I think there are explanations for this. First, we don't know how hard it is to make contact from the other side, or how much control a ghost has over their physical actions. What might seem like gently reaching out from a ghost's perspective could manifest on our side as a scratch. Second, some spirits are angry and afraid, and, just like living people, their emotions can get the best of them. Maybe they're not fundamentally bad people, but they are lashing out in reaction to their intense emotions or needs. A scratch could be a desperate attempt to better their own situation.

Amy and I talked rationally with this entity, telling them to stop harming our friend and that they couldn't harm anyone else. We laid our ground rules and stated our case in a firm, stern manner. This spirit didn't listen. It kept scratching our friend, and then we saw a large black mass crawl across the floor.

I don't know why—and you didn't see it on the episode—but in that moment, I felt the need to say the prayer to Saint Michael. Being in a centuries-old space in a city that has historically been nicknamed the "Holy City," I had a feeling that the area we were in had a Christian-based influence. "Saint Michael the Archangel, defend us in battle; be our protection against the wickedness and snares of the devil," I recited. "May God rebuke him, we humbly pray: and do thou, O Prince of the Heavenly Host, by the power of God, thrust into hell Satan and all the evil spirits who prowl about the world seeking the ruin of souls. Amen."

I didn't think that we were dealing with any sort of unholy spirit or demon by any means, but I suspected this prayer and intention would get a message across to whoever was causing harm to our friend. It was more formal than a prayer off the top of my head and conveyed a sense of authority. If they weren't going to listen to us telling them to stop, maybe they would at least respect our intentions through familiar text.

As soon as I finished, the energy of the space completely changed. Nothing else happened—no more scratches, and no more activity. Either they got the message and understood our point, or something divine had stepped in and made them stop. Maybe an angel swooped in and made the message clear, but I'd like to think that our intention set the tone.

Respecting Religion and Spiritual Boundaries

I will never pretend to know or try and access any religion beyond the one that I actually have a foundation in. I think it is a bit disrespectful to pull out a prayer book of a religion you haven't practiced and know nothing about. I am not Jewish and can't pretend to understand the Torah, and therefore I would consider it insensitive and disrespectful to try to use it myself during an investigation. Same for any organized religion like Islam, Hinduism, or Buddhism, or the beliefs of Indigenous peoples.

Sometimes while investigating, we need someone with expertise in belief systems with which we are unfamiliar. In these instances, we bring in someone affiliated with that particular religion to do the communicating. But it's not just about knowing the language and the spiritual practices involved. It's also a matter of authenticity, of possessing a spiritual energy that is firmly rooted in the belief system in question and has become a permanent fixture in their soul. That spirituality will make the process of healing more impactful.

There was a family case on season four of *Kindred Spirits* in Charleroi, Pennsylvania, where we had to call in others to assist in the healing that needed to take place to stop the activity. The father of the family had encountered a Native American entity in the woods on numerous occasions, describing them as looking like a warrior ready for battle. He felt very uncomfortable in the house and didn't want to assist with any outside work because he was afraid this Native spirit would be staring back at him.

The house abutted a beautiful natural creek, and the land had once belonged to the Seneca people. In 2011, the government built a pipeline that ran right though their yard. Amy and I, through our investigation, suspected the Native spirits were not happy with the addition of the pipeline, and were still fiercely trying to protect the land. It was our job to somehow let those spirits know that the current family had nothing to do with the further destruction of the land that they were defending.

We called in our friend Miguel Sague Jr., a shaman who has helped us achieve this type of healing connection for Indigenous entities in the past. Once he arrived, we went down to the creek where Miguel was able to connect with these spirits through ceremonial prayer and song. He had a strong feeling that whoever was there was angry, and they were still defending the creek. The Seneca people were fierce warriors and would fight to the death for their natural resources.

We wanted to unite the current owners of the land with the Seneca spirits. On the final day of the case, we gathered the family and Miguel together near the creek, where the most intense activity had occurred. Miguel performed a ceremony using native herbs and tobacco, along with chanting and song, to help connect the two worlds. He acted as a mediator between the spirit realm and the living in order to heal the wound that had been opened.

The family cared about the land and their home, and made it clear that they would protect that property just as fiercely. This healing would not have been possible without Miguel. For Amy and I to stand at the creek and tell the spirits that the family had nothing to do with any of the recent destruction of the area would fall on deaf ears. They would see us, and likely did see us, as being the same as those that caused the damage. However, Miguel was able to respectfully deliver this message, and offer prayers to facilitate peace and healing.

Almost immediately after the ritual we could feel the change that had taken place. It was as if the environment shifted. Amy was emotional during her final interview because the ceremony was so powerful. Miguel, who also has a strong psychic sense, was confident that the native spirits of that land now understood that the current family meant no harm. This was a few years ago and I haven't gotten any negative reports from the family. This is why it is so important, in some cases, to have the proper spiritual advisor to lead the way. It seems that both the living and the dead finally made peace.

PART TWO

Differing Perspectives on Death

CHAPTER 6

Death from a Ghost's Perspective

get asked a lot of questions about the paranormal, but the most frequent include:

"Is this stuff for real?"
"Have you really seen a ghost?"
"What is a ghost?"

I think the first two questions come from a place of skepticism and curiosity. Most people have never seen a ghost or had an experience, so I understand the queries. So, to get these questions out of the way: yes this "stuff" is for real, and yes, I have definitely seen a ghost. But the third question is harder to answer. Every time someone asks me what a ghost is, my mind spirals in a million different directions.

The Merriam-Webster definition of a ghost is, "a disembodied soul; especially: the soul of a dead person believed to be an inhabitant of the unseen world or to appear to the living in bodily likeness." That's a pretty good place to start. To me ghosts are energy. They can be residual (or non-intelligent) haunts, which I see as moments in time, memories brought to life through actions repeated over and over; or they can be interactive, intelligent haunts that can communicate with us and have their own thoughts and desires.

But the answer to that question at its core, for me, is a simple one. In basic terms, a ghost is someone who is no longer living on this earth, who was once in human form, and somehow can connect knowingly or unknowingly to the world around us. Even still, that's too complicated. Simply put, ghosts are people. That's the philosophy that drives everything Amy and I do. Ghosts were just like us, and now they are still just like us—but in their current state they are harder to hear, see, feel, and touch.

In my opinion it's better than what anyone in Hollywood could conjure up, because I believe a ghost comes to life in reality and can be observed and experienced by real people in real situations, not just in fictional scenarios on the screen. Ghosts have feelings and emotions. They can have problems and issues just like we have in everyday life. They have trouble communicating, sometimes they have trouble being around others, or expressing what they want. They can be the life of the party or the worst houseguest you could think of. They can take, give, manipulate, harass, and so much more. They are just like you and me, but in a sense, they're more complicated to deal with.

Much more confusing than what ghosts are, at least to me, is how and why they stay behind.

Why would anyone want to suffer our mortal dilemmas, and without the ability to communicate clearly or be seen by everyone?

There are a multitude of theories on the topic, but I like to focus on the reasons we get from spirits themselves. Some ghosts have a lot to say about their current situations in the afterlife. There can be many reasons why a spirit will stay behind, but I think they boil down to some fundamental desires we see most often. They're everything that we want when we are alive: need, desire, understanding, verbal communication, interaction, love, recognition, respect, connection, and remembrance. I don't think these are the only things a spirit can want, and by no means are spirits limited to a single trait. Often times, a spirit will show a lot of these characteristics based on the message they are trying to get across to the living.

However, the most common reason for manifestation is the idea of unfinished business. It's easy to see how not feeling accomplished or complete in life would inspire a spirit to linger. No matter how you depart from this earth, if in a sudden death or passing from a slow decline, you may have had more you wanted to achieve in your life. These feelings might be especially strong if you have time to contemplate your own passing, like with a prolonged sickness. You essentially have to go through the stages of grief with your own mortality.

I am aware that there are those who come to terms with their own passing by the time they cross over, but through our investigations, we've spoken to many spirits who time and time again say they had so many other things they wanted to do while they were alive. A huge source of unfinished business is family situations. Sometimes we see people who remain with loved ones so they can watch over them. We also see spirits who regret not mending a burned bridge, or losing touch with a loved one they didn't reconnect with before they passed. To me, this is one of the saddest situations we encounter when we connect with those in the afterlife. I guess that's why there are so many sayings like carpe diem and no day but today, and countless songs about living today like it's your last.

Ghosts Who Stay Behind to Heal Spiritual Trauma

One of the most striking examples of spirits staying behind for family—and one that was incredibly powerful for me as an investigator—was at the Fee House in Little Rock, Arkansas. Amy and I were there for a season six episode of *Kindred Spirits*.

The former home of one of the most prominent families in Little Rock, the Fee House is shrouded in mystery, speculation, and death. The house as it stands today is still a picture of 19th century grandeur, but years of abandonment have discolored the walls, caused cracks in the plaster, and left all but forgotten ghosts of the former family to roam the halls of what was once a place of decadence.

The Fee family had seen its share of scandal while family members were living at the home. Mamie Kone and Frank Fee were both newly divorced form their respective spouses when they got together and they married each other almost immediately after their previous marriages ended. Thomas, their fourth son, was rumored to be fathered by the servant who cared for the house and grounds. Frank passed in 1922 from a heart attack while out of town on business; Mamie Fee died horrifically nine years later, in 1931.

Mamie's granddaughter, Patricia, who was eight or nine at the time, witnessed her grandmother's accident, and recalled the scene to Abandoned Arkansas, writing to them in an email: "We had an open grate (for heating the room) and my grandmother had washed her hair and she was in her nightgown drying her hair over the stove. Her gown caught fire—the maid, Amelia, was the only one with her—she rolled her in a blanket, to smother the flames. She was burned—she would tell no one. Edward [Mamie's third child] was to be married at that time, and she didn't want to spoil his marriage plans, so she kept her plight to herself. After the wedding she got so bad, she did go to a hospital for the burns, but it was too late. From this she died. She was a good Christian Scientist—many the time she would call someone to pray that I would get well. Maybe that, too, was a reason she didn't go to the hospital sooner."

Less than a year later, Katherine, who was Mamie's daughter and Patricia's mom, also suffered a terrible fate in the house. Katherine drank poison on the grand staircase while her husband and two brothers looked on. Contemporary newspaper accounts spun a tale of accidental death; the official story was that she had a headache, and to remedy the pain, she accidentally took poison instead of painkillers. Patricia, her daughter, recounts a very different story. She recalls her mother and uncles arguing about who was to blame for the recent death of their mother. Katherine blamed her brother and claimed he had "lost the faith." In the midst of this argument, Katherine deliberately went upstairs, found the acid, and drank it intentionally as she was standing above the family on the staircase, causing her almost immediate and horrific death. Grief is a strong motivator and can manifest itself in many ways. I don't believe Katherine had a strong family support system and so she relied heavily on her faith. She tested God, and believed if she had strong faith, he would save her. She drank the poison and died. According to the Bible, it is unacceptable to test God when it's rooted in doubt. I believe her grief clouded her judgment and swayed her to contradict what she had been taught.

When new owners purchased the house a century later, they immediately started experiencing intense activity. They saw the shadow figure of a man whom they believed to be Frank Fee; large bangs resounded around the house; and someone saw the apparition of a female standing behind them while they were looking into an upstairs mirror.

So, Amy and I set out to find out who was haunting this location and if there was anything we could do to mitigate the situation. One late evening we decided to employ the Estes Method, created by our friends Connor Randall, Karl Pfeiffer, and Michelle Tate. For this investigation technique, one investigator listens to a spirit box, which uses the white noise of radio static, flipping through frequencies to allow spirit voices to come through. The investigator also wears noise canceling headphones and a blindfold, so as to not see their surroundings or read any lips. The other investigator asks questions while the listener relays the answers they hear from the box.

The goal of this method is to create a situation where the listener is an unbiased translator of information. They have no idea what the other investigator is asking, only relaying what they hear in the headphones; if the questions and answers match up, theoretically, a spirit is communicating and having a conversation with the investigator asking questions.

There are a few reasons why we implement this technique during our investigations.

The original purpose and use of the spirit box is to play it out loud so everyone can hear it. Paranormal investigators believe that spirits can manipulate the sweeping radio frequency and create words and phrases which we hear. The Estes Method takes it much further than that, allowing the person who is immersed in the audio to become a conduit. Through sensory deprivation, it creates a meditative state that allows an investigator to more clearly understand the sprit messages. I personally believe there is a strong psychic element involved. When using the spirit box the original way, you may hear a word or phrase and then craft your own assumptions about what is being said.

When I am doing the Estes Method, I sometimes hear a word or phrase skipping through the static but mostly I *feel* the need to say the word or phrase. I also, at times, connect emotionally with the spirit and can sense their fear, anger, frustration, excitement, and can describe that to others who are investigating. Their emotions sometimes take over my own; I can still function as myself but I know that what I am sensing is not of my own doing, as if their energy is intertwining with mine for a brief period of time. Lastly, I've received visuals that I feel are scenes from what this spirit has witnessed. All of these things better inform our investigation in as neutral a way as possible and give us substantially better results than listening to the spirit box out loud. We do all of this to add an extra layer of scrutiny to our evidence. If we put all of our controls in place, the things we capture and the experiences we have are that much more astonishing.

In this session, we made contact with Katherine. Right away, she brought up the very subject I didn't want to ask about. "The poison was painful," she said, as relayed by Amy.

"Okay Katherine, please talk to us," I said. I was the one asking the questions, and Amy was receiving the answers. "The poison, the painfulness of it, did you mean to do that? Did you mean to drink that poison?"

"Actually. Careful. Listen," she said.

"Yes?" I responded.

"ACID."

"I get it, okay," I replied. "Acid." But I wanted to know something else.

"They said it was an accident. Is that true?"

"Family," Katherine said. "There are things that we can't say, we whisper."

Obviously, Katherine was talking about family secrets. From this exchange it seems that Katherine's daughter Patricia's story was correct, that Katherine drank the poison on purpose and the family did everything they could to cover it up.

We were on to something. We continued our investigation, and discovered that Mamie, her mother, was also coming through our recorder, answering questions via EVP. She communicated that she felt sorry for her daughter, and that she wasn't with Katherine in the afterlife. It was so strange—the two spirits were in the house, but they weren't together.

The next morning, we reviewed our DVR cameras. I noticed that there was a weird disturbance in Mamie's room. The footage showed what looked like a white misty shadow figure coming from the landing where Amy had been sitting earlier for our Estes session, moving toward the room where Mamie had been set on fire—but before it crossed the frame of the door, it vanished, as though it couldn't go past the threshold.

We had to find a way to connect the mother and daughter in the afterlife in order for them to communicate with each other. We were curious to understand why they weren't aware of each other's presence in the house, or, in the event they were aware, why they couldn't communicate with each other. Most importantly, there seemed to be some unresolved family trauma that had spilled over in to the afterlife. Maybe that was the reason why they were in the same place but somehow never crossed paths. We wanted to reconnect a mother and daughter to provide closure, peace, and reconciliation.

We felt that there were two separate hauntings happening, but they somehow overlapped each other and that's what was causing such intense activity in the house. There was Katherine's space and then there was Mamie's space. The solution was that Amy and I were going to go upstairs and sit, splitting the distance between where we got communication from Katherine and Mamie. We would each independently be a receiver on a spirit box in Estes Method sessions, each of us focusing on a different spirit. We let Katherine know that she could speak through Amy as she had done earlier, and told Mamie that she could use the device I was holding to speak through me.

While blindfolded and in headphones, Amy and I would have no idea what was happening during this experience. She and I were relaying what we heard, but we couldn't hear what the other was saying, only learning what was said when we played back the footage. Our hope was that even though the women didn't realize they were both occupying the same space, we would open a channel of communication for them and they would become aware of each other. Afterall, they both could see and hear Amy and me. Would Katherine and Mamie finally notice each other and communicate after all these years?

"Speak out," Mamie said through me immediately.

"I'm surprised," Katherine said through Amy. "Of all the people."

"Do you remember?" Mamie asked. A beat. A pause. "Purple flowers?"

"Yes," Katherine answered.

"We had to be a certain way," Mamie said.

I can see how something as simple and visually beautiful as purple flowers could spark a shared memory. It could have also been that Mamie was asking Katherine about those flowers to make sure it really was her daughter.

"Mom?" Katherine said. "You are in heaven."

I'm not sure how Katherine could know that—maybe by the energy Mamie was giving off. This statement made me believe that Mamie was a spirit who could come and go, who might not be in the space all the time. That could be a reason they never crossed paths.

Mamie seemed freer, but Katherine seemed stuck. I've seen situations before where, when someone dies of suicide, it's as if they are confined to the space and time where the act took place, and they relive bits of it over and over until one day they are somehow able to free themselves.

"I know that," Mamie said, seemingly confirming that she existed in a plane she considered heaven. But she had more to say about what Katherine had done.

"I can't condone," Mamie said. "You deserve to die." I heard Mamie sigh, and felt the weight of her sadness and disappointment. That sense of emotion is another reason we find the Estes Method to be such a useful investigative tool.

Even in the afterlife, it seemed, Mamie still held to the belief that what Katherine did was a sin. What's so interesting is that Mamie was fully aware of what her daughter did, even though she passed away before her daughter. She acknowledged that she has an awareness of our world even if she isn't always earthbound. That idea has bigger implications for when and how some spirits choose to interact. Those moments when we *feel* that a deceased loved one is with us, maybe they really are.

"It's true," Katherine said, acknowledging their shared religious belief.

"Tell her now.... Why?" Mamie asked.

"I just had to do it," Katherine responded. Amy said that she heard crying, then: "Never again please.... You're killing me.... Stop."

Mamie said in response, "I'll always care."

That was it. It was powerful and utterly profound. In this one conversation, we observed the existence of two spirits in the afterlife, both on separate planes. The one who died of suicide was regretful. Her mother, on the other hand, was still a maternal figure, not condoning what her daughter had done, but also letting her know that she would always care about her. Most importantly, this experiment worked. By providing a method of communication they had never had before, we connected two ghosts in the same house who were not aware of each other, and we brought a family back together so that they could heal their relationship and try to move on. I don't know if Katherine is still stuck in that house, but I believe what we did helped start the healing and I hope she has found some peace.

Ghosts Who Stay Behind for Living Family

In an episode on season three of *Kindred Spirits*, we encountered a spirit who was staying behind to try to help heal the relationship between her mother and her sister. Sharon, the mother, strongly believed that an evil entity was living in her home, and had been tormenting and following her for years. Sharon had two living children, a daughter Anna and a son Brady. She had also lost two children, most recently her oldest daughter, Miranda, who had been killed in a horrible accident involving a negligent driver.

Anna was living in the basement in Miranda's old room. Her relationship with Sharon seemed to be on the rocks. The energy in the basement bedroom was strong and we were guessing from our investigation up to that point that the older sister may have still been lingering around the house. We thought perhaps the activity the family was experiencing seemed so intense because she had something to say—a message to get across to the family—but was being misunderstood.

We started to engage with Miranda during one of our EVP sessions by letting her know we understood the position she was in. "No one can see you, and no one can hear you," Amy said. "But we can try with what we've brought here. We can try to see you and hear you."

"I'm right here," we heard Miranda say. She told us that she believed we could fix what was happening in the house. Miranda and her mother were not on good terms when she passed away suddenly, so there was a lot of unfinished business, sorrow, and loss connected to this haunting. Sharon was clearly living with and grappling with her grief, but Miranda was doing the same thing in the afterlife. And Miranda saw the same tension happening between Sharon and Anna that she had experienced with her mother: they were at odds, and their relationship was heading downhill very quickly.

Sharon had to be a part of the conversation; it was her responsibility to try and heal the relationship and make things right with her daughters, both living and dead. We decided to bring Sharon to Miranda's old room so that the two of them could make amends and try to work through some of their grief together. We gave her a K2 meter, a device that reads electromagnetic frequency levels. Theoretically, a spirit can manipulate this device and make the lights change color as they interact with it.

Amy started the conversation by saying, "We know you're down here. We talked to you. We brought your mom. Is this what you want us to do to fix things here?" At that moment, the K2 meter Sharon was holding lit up.

"Do you want your mom and Anna to have a loving relationship?" Amy asked. When we played back the EVP recording, we all heard, "I do."

Then it was Sharon's turn to speak. I said, "What do you want to say?"

She took a moment and then said, "I love her. I love her a lot. I miss her. I'm sorry for what happened to her and I am fighting for her every day." The K2 meter lit up again. "She's my girl," Sharon said. "She's still my girl."

After a few moments, I said, "Miranda, I know you are here to help facilitate this and we do appreciate you being here helping us with this task because it is very important. And when you are ready to go, you can go."

Again, the K2 meter lit up, but even more brightly than before. We were all moved with emotion as Miranda let us know that she understood. Then we heard footsteps upstairs. The sound made its way over our heads to where the front door of the home was. We were stunned to silence. No one was upstairs at the time.

"Maybe she was leaving," Amy said. I asked for Miranda to reach out to us again if she was still there, but everything had gone dark. No sound, no lights from the equipment, no voices from our recorder. Miranda accomplished her unfinished business and then left in peace, healing her family from the other side.

Four years later, I reached out to Sharon. I wanted to know what happened after we investigated, and more about her experience over the ensuing years. Physically, she looked exactly the same as the last time we saw each other, only this time there seemed to be a lightness to her.

"You know, that initial phone call was devastating," she said. "You're completely numb and then the funeral is over and that's when there's no getting out of it. There's just this dark cloud that encompasses you, and you have to learn to grieve. You have to grieve, but don't let it overcome you and don't let it overtake you. Grieving is healthy, grieving is normal. Grieving is human."

Sharon said being able to talk to Miranda that night "helped immensely" with her grief and regret. "There's not very many parents that get to hear their deceased daughter, after she's gone, give a message," she said. "That was amazing."

She got confirmation and direct communication from the afterlife that Miranda was okay and that she forgave her. "In that moment I felt like something got lifted," Sharon explained. "I felt lighter. I was so happy to know that we were on good terms and it took a load off of me." She isn't experiencing panic attacks anymore, and Brady, who still resides with his mom, isn't afraid to be in the house either.

"Anna and I have gotten along so good in the last couple of years," she added. "We get along great. We love each other. There are no bad feelings, no arguing, nothing." The work she and Anna did together, she said, "repaired our relationship, so it didn't go any further like it got with Miranda."

The goal every time we do any investigation is to help both the living and the dead. When we are dealing with a family it becomes even more important; sometimes the pressure of getting it right is overwhelming. We don't ever want to make anything worse by causing more fear and anxiety over a situation. While we know we can't do the healing for them, and we're not mental health professionals by any means, we always try to make a positive impact. Sharon's words affirmed for me that what we are doing, at this moment in the paranormal, is exactly what we should be doing. We make a difference every single time, and this testimony, after the family had a couple of years to grow and continue the work, is indeed humbling.

We have witnessed many such instances of a spirit reaching out to a loved one to help them through a difficult time. In an episode of season two of *Kindred Spirits* when we were investigating the Lizzie Borden House in Fall River, Massachusetts, we were trying to get to the source of paranormal activity in the house, and were investigating with a longtime employee, Sue.

In an EVP session, the spirit made it clear they didn't want to talk to either me or Amy. Then Sue realized it might be her deceased grandfather trying to communicate with her directly.

"Pepe," she asked, "was that you trying to talk to me? Does somebody up here have a message for me?"

"Yes," the spirit responded. It was her deceased grandfather. "Let go."

After hearing those responses on the recorder, Sue told us something we hadn't previously known. Her father was currently in hospice care, and wasn't expected to live much longer. Even though we had no idea we would be talking to Sue's grandfather or that her family was attached to any of the activity, he came through from wherever he was to let her know that everything was going to be okay. She didn't have to hold onto the pain and grief she was feeling. She could let go and focus on the time she and her father still had together. She mentioned to us that he spoke of being ready to go on to the next journey. This affirmation gave Sue comfort and enabled her to be completely present with him to the very end, rather than retreating into her own sorrow and grief.

Ghosts Who Stay Behind Because They Can't, or Don't Want to, Let Go

When you spend your life working towards something, it only makes sense that you want to hold onto it as long as you can—and sometimes, we encounter spirits who do that long into the afterlife.

These spirits are some of the most aggressive we encounter, and most of them have the mentality that everything should be done according to their specifications and their plans. We've had many cases in the past where the person we are reaching out to had, one way or another, achieved their own version of the American dream—and once they died they wanted to make sure that what they had built or achieved continued to thrive.

During season one of *Kindred Spirits*, Amy and I visited the home of a family in New Britain, Connecticut. The building used to be classified as a single-family home but had subsequently been divided into three separate apartments; one sister and her son lived on the third floor, the other sister and her young son lived on the second floor, and the grandmother lived on the first.

They were experiencing aggressive activity. The youngest of the two kids, who was five, talked about seeing a shadow figure at night when he was in bed trying to sleep. Also, they were so frightened that entire sections of the apartments were not even being used. Their father had died thirteen years prior but the intense activity didn't match up to who they knew their father to be.

Through our research, we found that the building was constructed in 1920s and was purchased in the 1950s by a Mr. Kotek, who immigrated to America from Poland in the hopes of building a better life for his family. During our initial EVP sessions, we weren't getting much of a response from any of our questions. But finally, Amy asked, "Is there anyone in this room with us? Whoever you are, can you tell me your name?"

"Ko-tek," we faintly made out from the recording.

"We are looking for anyone who lived in this house," Amy continued. "Are you Mr. Kotek?"

The answer was a very clear "Yes."

We kept questioning him, but we didn't get any further response at all. The next day, Amy reached out to living relatives of Mr. Kotek—of the many things we learned about him and the life he built for his family, we found out that neither he nor his wife spoke any English. We needed a translator.

Since we were just up the hill from the Little Poland area of town, a member of our crew ventured out to a local Polish restaurant, asking if there was anyone who would be willing to translate for some ghost hunters. The co-owner Margaret, as luck would have it, was interested in the paranormal and was happy to help us. Even better, she had grown up in Poland and knew a lot about the history of the community.

Back in the attic of the home, Margaret translated our questions for us. "Do you want to stay here?" she asked in Polish.

"He said 'tak,'" Margaret said. "It means 'yes' in Polish."

She asked him where he worked, and when he answered the Atlantic Tool Factory, we knew we were on the right track. We asked her to translate one final question: "Is this your home?"

His answer was an emphatic "NO." It made sense. The home had been changed so much, and, at the time we investigated, was in a state of disarray from renovations and moving. There were boxes and construction material all around. Indeed, it was no longer his home, especially not in that condition.

Margaret got very excited at that point, and had goosebumps all over her body. She said that it would make so much sense that he would say it was no longer his home, because there is a Polish saying that means "order has to be." The home he worked so hard for, if he were still alive, would not be in the condition it was presently in. But we were confident that once the renovations were over and the home was put back in order, he would be able to see that his dream wasn't being forgotten and his legacy would continue to be remembered for many decades to come. The family took this idea one step further. We all went back to the attic and with the help of our translator, Margaret, each person was able to speak with Mr. Kotek directly. They assured him that they would be following through and taking care of his home and property.

Ghosts Who Don't Want to Be Forgotten

Let's be real, no one wants to fade into obscurity, with no one to remember their names or think back on them fondly. Imagine being dead and trying to hold on to the hope your memory won't be tossed aside—then in trying to keep your legacy alive, you are unknowingly scaring the crap out of the new owners of your house because you just want to be acknowledged.

In season two of *Kindred Spirits*, Amy and I were called to a home in Somersworth, New Hampshire. It was a total mystery to us—although a bank teller had been murdered nearby, none of the activity seemed to be connected to that, or to anyone who previously owned or currently owned the home.

We eventually found out that the homeowners had a tombstone in the backyard, salvaged from a discard pile that they had found when they moved in. It had been placed in the backyard by the previous owner to stop her dog from digging under the fence. When we looked into the name on the stone, we discovered it was a World War II veteran who was buried in a cemetery nearby—only the tombstone on his grave had his name misspelled. The stone in the backyard was the correct version. It turned out he was haunting the family to get them to realize the mistake and to correct it by taking the replacement headstone to his final resting place. We contacted his living relatives and they took the stone to his grave. The activity has stopped since then.

Similarly, we've also met ghosts who stick around because they take issue with the way they're remembered. This was the case with an episode on season four of *Kindred Spirits*, at the Old St. Johns County Jail in St. Augustine, Florida. Many people were executed for their crimes there, but one man who was hanged was definitely innocent. In our investigation, we had gotten an EVP that said, "I'm not a murderer," which led us down a path of trying to find someone who had been wrongly convicted. In our research, we found the story of Jim Kirby and Robert Lee. The men were tried and convicted of murder in 1901 and sentenced to death. But on the day they were to be executed, Kirby confessed that Lee had nothing to do with the crime—but he wasn't able to save the other man.

Before he was hanged, Lee made this statement to a reporter: "Yes sir, I am innocent, but I am not lying. I am going to meet death bravely. I know God will deal justly with me and I have no fears for the result after death. I am dying happy. I know the public believes I am guilty and that I have been cursed and abused, but I am innocent, and you will learn such in the next world if not in this."

By causing so much activity in the jail that someone finally listened to him, Lee was able to clear his name publicly. I hope that, by knowing people finally understand that he was innocent, he's been able to find some closure in his afterlife, wherever that might be.

Ghosts Who Simply Don't Want to Leave

As many reasons as we can uncover for why spirits stay behind, sometimes it boils down to the fact that they simply don't want to go. Maybe they don't want to be forgotten, or maybe they just miss their lives and what they loved to do. I've encountered those in the afterlife who are just content to continue to live in their homes as if nothing had happened to them or nothing had changed.

During season seven of *Kindred Spirits*, we went to Bellefonte, Pennsylvania, to investigate a home. The homeowner, Sarah, had moved sight unseen into the house, and she and all three of her kids were seeing apparitions and experiencing strong activity.

When we made contact with the spirit, we found that it was the previous owner of the home: a woman named Nancy who had a strong desire not to leave her house. She passed away suddenly one morning and her spirit still lingered.

In an Estes session, Amy was asking her why she chose to stay, and I was listening for responses. "When we know, we'll go," Nancy said through me. I don't know if she was talking about all spirits and ghosts as a collective "we," or if she saw that idea as collective consciousness, but it seemed to me that she was just speaking for herself. She will go when she knows to go.

Then she continued, "I have final words." She paused, then said, "I miss it."

"What do you miss?" Amy asked.

"Life, my life…before I was in the ground…with memories of the birds," Nancy replied. It was so incredibly moving to hear. We had made a strong enough connection to this person that she felt she could share her deepest fear or sorrow about her current situation.

Nancy had one final, beautiful statement to impart to us. "The world is wide," she said. "Love is strong. Tell them they don't need to be afraid. Those are the words. Now I'm gonna stop."

With that she didn't say another word. She left all of it on the table for us to hear and process. It truly felt like a gift to get a small glimmer into what it may feel like to be where she is. I know that every spirit has a different circumstance, but I also know that there are some common human experiences among spirits we communicate with. They speak about love, loss, and the simple idea that we are all one and are all connected.

Ghosts Who Don't Know They're Dead

We don't know for certain if any of these ghosts in the situations I've discussed above actively *chose* to stay behind, or whether they just chose to make the best of the situation and do some good because they still existed on this plane. In any case, it almost seems as though those spirits are defying death. Despite no longer being alive, they're still growing as individuals.

The harder spirits to understand are the ones who don't know they've passed away. This was the case with Wilhelmina Crocker in season three of *Kindred Spirits*. We were investigating the Crocker Tavern House—an 18th century inn turned private home of my dear friend Kate and her husband Joe in Barnstable, Massachusetts—and we couldn't find any explanation for the unusually strong activity in the home.

When visiting early on, the pair knew there was some paranormal activity, but didn't think anything serious of it. "When we first bought the house, I was four weeks pregnant," Kate told me recently. "There were little bits and pieces of activity, but nothing too extreme. And we were only there for a few days after we signed the contract to buy the house," because they returned to California, where they were living at the time.

It wasn't until she and her husband brought their newborn son, Michael, back to the house that the space became more active and she began to be genuinely concerned with what unseen entity was in her home. "As we started spending time there, that's when the activity started to ramp up," she said. "Having a newborn, I started to feel pretty unsafe having all this stuff happening."

Once, in the middle of the night, Kate saw an apparition of a man running towards her in her bedroom. "I screamed and said, 'Stop, stop, stop.' My husband convinced me it was a dream, but I was like, 'I have to sell this house if I can't sleep in this house.' I was terrified." That's when Kate reached out to me for help. And I will be honest, I was nervous about it. She needed immediate help, and we were in the middle of filming a season, so the only way I could get to her anytime soon was to use the house in an episode of *Kindred*. The prospect of not fixing a problem so severe it made my friend want to sell her house put a unique level of stress on the situation. We had to get it right, and the pressure, at least for me, was more than any other case we had done up to that point.

Eventually, we learned that a woman named Wilhelmina, or Willie for short, married into the Crocker family and had lived in a home nearby. In 1926, she had died in a terrible accident, when her car was struck by a train. Her spirit, as far as we could surmise, was attracted to the tavern because the historic building looked the same as it did when she was alive, so it was familiar to her.

We did an experiment in which Amy went to the site of her death, and I stayed at the Crocker Tavern, conducting the Estes Method, while Amy asked questions with her recorder and directed Wilhelmina to interact with me at the house. The results were powerful: Amy had an intense experience where all the train lights and alarms went off, even though no train was coming to the crossing, while I heard the sounds of a crash in the house at the same time.

What we realized in talking to Wilhelmina, though, was that she didn't understand that she had died in the crash.

"I went to the train tracks where you were killed," Amy said in an EVP session. "Did you see me there?"

"Yes," we heard back.

"Can you tell us who Clarence Shirley Crocker is?"

"My husband," Willie responded.

"It's almost a hundred years since you passed away," Amy said.

"No," Willie said. She didn't know she had died and didn't want to face the truth. We had to show her proof.

"Can you read this?" Amy asked. "I'm just bringing it here to show you that it's your death certificate."

"Death certificate?" Willie asked.

"Tell us what you want us to do," Amy said.

"I'm going home," Willie responded.

"Mrs. Crocker, I know this is hard," Amy said, "but we'll make sure no one forgets you, okay?"

We didn't hear from Willie again. I think she must have known on some level that she had passed, but that us talking to her about it triggered something that finally allowed her to see her circumstance. I can't imagine how hard it was for her to be shown her own death certificate—but I can only hope that she found her way home, as she wanted to.

My research and work have led me to more questions than answers at this point. It seems to me that the majority of spirits who stick around do so by their own intention, and those that had no say in where they find themselves after death seem to be okay with their situation for the most part. I don't know if we can choose to stay behind. I do know that the will of the human mind and soul is that powerful. Maybe our wants and needs are so strong that they allow us to continue our own worldly pursuits in this world even in the afterlife.

For the sake of child spirits, I hope we have a choice in the matter. Interacting and helping children who have passed on, but remain in spirit, is one of the most difficult things to cope with as an investigator, because you are dealing with the innocence of a child. To be forced into living as a ghost without your consent or knowledge as an adult is frightening, but for this to happen as a child must be utterly terrifying. We've had cases in the past where we communicate with the spirits of children, and sometimes they are confused about where they are. Some know where their parents are, while others do not. Thinking any child has passed and may be lingering on the other side lost, alone, and frightened makes me want to work even harder to find out why some of us continue in a ghostly form.

My dear friend and paranormal researcher John E.L. Tenney has discussed a theory that we have the ability to manifest our own destiny based on our belief system. For instance, if you are religious and believe in heaven, the theory says, then when you die you go to somewhere heavenly. If you believe in nothing, then after you pass there will be nothing. If you are agnostic, maybe you get a chance to figure it out once you pass or incidentally maybe that's what some call purgatory. In that same vein, if you believe in ghosts and lingering spirits, could you then in turn make yourself stick around as a ghost after you have passed?

That line of thinking gives the power of our eternal life back to us, and allows us the ability to not only hope a certain thing happens to us after we go, but to manifest it. The question remains: would I choose to be a ghost or not when the end comes? And what if, by considering the option now, we are manifesting that future for ourselves? It's a heady topic. Best not to decide definitively now, at least for me. I can't put all my paranormal eggs into one basket. There's still too much to learn about the unknown.

CHAPTER 7

Death from the Living's Perspective

Living with paranormal activity can be frightening, especially if you don't fully grasp why it might be happening. It's only natural to be afraid of what we don't understand. Believe it or not, we have a role in the hauntings we find in our homes...and not all of the activity is caused by ghosts. Sometimes our minds can run wild and play tricks on us, especially if we are frightened or anxious. You could be sitting at home and hear a noise down the hall. Most of us would probably not even notice it—but if you already think your house is haunted, you'll immediately assume that sound is a ghost. It might be, but it also might just be a terrestrial noise and your imagination is conjuring up other explanations. A month down the road, you might assume the worst possible scenario...the house settling or the mouse in the attic, in your mind, is now an angry spirit trying to wreak havoc on your life and family. The anxiety of what could be runs away with your logical mind and you can't see past your own fear.

When we investigate a case, we examine all possibilities and explanations for activity, both paranormal and not—and we often discuss with clients that their energy and intention have some influence over what's happening in their home. We provide those that we help, both living and nonliving, with tools to better process and understand the activity that may still continue in their home. The dead—no matter what we say and do—think and act their own way. We help the living understand that, and in turn humanize the haunt while giving them confidence to not be afraid anymore.

That's what we hoped for when Amy and I left Kate and Joe at Crocker Tavern: that we were able to give them some peace of mind. But we would later learn that the activity was far from over. When we left, they reported experiencing minimal activity for a while. About sixteen months after we filmed our episode there, things were so intense in the home that they called the police.

By then, they were a family of four, with a three-year-old son Michael and an eight-month-old daughter, Lulu. On the night of the police call, they had just arrived back in town, and they were all sleeping in the room—known as Aunt Lydia's Room—where Kate had seen the apparition of the man. "Around 2:00 a.m., I started hearing bangs in the hallway," she said. "I heard heavy footsteps, and a door slam. And I woke Joe up, saying, 'There's someone in the hallway, there's something in the hallway.' His feeling was that someone had broken into the house, or someone was living in the house because it was a seasonal house."

If someone knew they only used the property seasonally, they could easily squat in the home in a different wing, and Kate and her family might not have noticed for at least a day or two. But she felt differently than her husband did. "I knew immediately it was a ghost," she told me. Then, there was a second door slam. They called the police.

"There must have been like ten people outside of our house at that point," Kate recalled. "And, of course, the fire department comes too, because we're a historic house. Everybody was there. We were talking to them through the windows because it was the pandemic. They said, 'Don't leave your room, you're safe in there.'"

While the family stayed in that bedroom, first responders looked through the whole house, including the eaves and the attic, but there was nothing. "Then one of the older cops said to my husband, 'Hey, have you experienced any ghost activity in this house? Because I've been sent here many, many times over the years.'" The officer explained that over his decades on the force, he had been sent to the house numerous times for unexplained activity, and no one was ever there.

When friends ask me about what to do in situations like this, I try to give the same advice I would give anyone else: You must take control of what is happening, take control of your own house, and make sure these entities—familiar or not—know that you are in charge, that it is your house, and that you will not be taking any crap from anyone, dead or alive. It's about setting your boundaries as a living person and making sure those that are still there, who are non-living, understand the rules that you set forth. With all due respect, of course.

"I was still shaking, but we went to sit at the top of the stairs," Kate said. "We told the ghosts, 'We are going to live here full-time now. This is going to be our home.' That was a very scary night."

I asked her whether she thought she could have been open to that kind of communication before everything happened with Wilhelmina Crocker. "Absolutely not," she said. "No way. I think watching the way that you and Amy dealt with everything and talked to the spirits like they were people, with feelings—and how sad you both were when you had to explain to Wilhelmina that she was dead—kind of made spirits more vulnerable and accessible and not so scary to me."

I've said it before and I will say it again: The humanization of spirits is the only way we can better understand the activity that is happening. Hearing something like this, from someone we helped, who is a dear friend, validated the work that we do more than you can imagine.

Once you understand where the activity is coming from, not the actual location, but the intention behind the ghostly outburst, it can flip the way you feel about the spirits that are still in your house. Some people even start to consider them part of the family.

In season six of *Kindred Spirits*, we went to Angola, New York, to investigate activity so extreme that Missy and her family were afraid of their own home. Any changes they tried to make to the house were met with intense backlash from unseen forces. "I felt like I was being stalked in my own house," she said. Missy was afraid to go into her sewing room in the basement, where she would make beautiful quilts, because she always felt on edge there. She had heard her name being called, been touched by a cold unseen hand, and seen her sewing machine turn on by itself, just to name a few. She would turn on loud music so she could drown out any strange noises. One day, she was cutting fabric and she could just feel someone standing in the doorway and had to immediately leave. She was so upset that from then on, she completely avoided going down to her workspace.

She also wouldn't go into the attic because she heard a rumor that someone had hanged themselves there and she would hear the sound of people coming from the attic when nobody was around. "It was horrible. Horrible," she said. "I just would think, oh my gosh, the bad energy has to be up there. I felt it every time I went up there—somebody didn't want me there. You see all the horror movies of people that die these horrible deaths, and I'm thinking I'm going to come up here and find some grotesque bent neck man walking around."

However, it was all a story, a rumor. Death records confirmed that there was never a suicide in the house. Her fear of thinking the suicide by hanging could be true, coupled with all of the intense paranormal activity that was happening in her home, affected her and made everything more intense and frightening. She was aware of the ghostly footsteps and sounds coming from the attic at all times of the day. Her fear of going up the steps and confronting it, and also possibly seeing something that she couldn't un-see related to the suicide, made a portion of her home off limits.

In our investigation, we made contact with a deceased Polish couple, Stephan and Emilia, who had previously owned the house and wanted the place kept the same as it had been during their lifetimes. Once Missy knew that it was just a family who loved the house as much as she did, everything changed.

Catching up with Missy two years after our investigation, she said that understanding who the ghosts in her home are has totally changed her perspective on living in a haunted house. "I have found since the investigation, now that I know who's here, I'm so incredibly protective of them," said Missy. When we talked, she was sitting in her quilt room, an area of her home she previously hated being in because of the activity. At this point, she had completely changed her views on the unseen spirits that she had previously found so frightening.

"I have this fierce loyalty to them," Missy explained. "People ask if they can investigate my house, and I say no, because I don't know if someone's going to be cruel, and come in and be disrespectful to them or upset them even more."

People say if they were in her shoes, they'd sell the house—but she feels totally the opposite now. "I can't turn them over to somebody I don't know. Does that sound ridiculous? I talk to them so much more now, like it's an everyday occurrence," she said. "I feel like they are more obvious when they're trying to get my attention to things now than they were before the investigation. Now that those lines of communication have been opened, we have a dialogue, which we didn't have before."

Missy has even asked their opinion on renovations to the home. Her eighty-one-year-old mother, a devout Catholic, has never been afraid of the ghosts in the home—in fact, she asked to come spend more time at the house. So, they had an idea to renovate her son's old room into a room for her mother. Missy said, "My mom's like, 'You know, I would really like to be able to come out and stay,' even though my brothers are saying, 'You're crazy, you know what goes on out there?' But she's not afraid. She loves this house."

So while they were working on the attic—something they had been afraid to do before—Missy asked Stephan to chime in on the changes she wanted to make for her mother's new space. Missy took her own EMF detector and sat down on the floor in her son's old room. (As mentioned earlier, an EMF detector reads levels of electromagnetic frequency, which often amp up when spirits are nearby.)

"I said out loud to Stephan, 'Now listen, my mom needs a place to stay. You've dealt with her before. She doesn't take your crap, but we're gonna make this room into a spare room for her.' I asked him: 'Do you think I should rip up this floor and put some laminate in?' And nothing happened. No response on the EMF detector. And then when I said, 'Well, maybe we should sand the floor and refinish it and bring it back to its former glory." And right away that EMF went nuts." So that's what Missy did.

"I love that Stephan and I can do it together," she said.

Missy has come so far from our initial investigation of her property. So has Kate. Both have a deeper understanding of what was happening in their homes, and ways to deal with the fear of the unknown.

Kate's husband Joe is Catholic. He didn't believe in ghosts, and thought all the activity they were having in their home on Cape Cod was explainable through things that weren't paranormal. It wasn't until he started having more experiences that he accepted there was activity in his home. He has now turned to religion as a way to deal with the issues that occur in the home.

"My son will call out in the middle of the night and say there's a ghost, and my husband will run out of the bedroom with holy water and like, spray it," Kate said. "If you see this six-foot-three man fly out of bed with holy water in the middle of the night...it's impressive. He's in that room in seconds." At Joe's request, they also had a priest come in and bless the house.

I think what's interesting is Joe immediately turned to religion as a buffer and for his own peace of mind. The way that ghosts and religion intersect is an interesting conundrum. If the spirits Joe is encountering aren't Catholic, his holy water and his prayers likely won't have any effect on them. But the intention of the action is to provide protection and safety. As long as he feels comforted by those actions, it's probably improving the situation, regardless of the direct effect on the spirits present.

Maybe it does work. Maybe the intention of him doing what he thinks is best according to his beliefs makes the spirits stop and think that they might have gone a step too far. It's the same concept as Kate going to sit in the hallway and taking a stand, setting boundaries with a conversation. But I think it's really interesting that Kate has gone from being afraid of what was happening, to handling it—while her husband went from not believing in any paranormal activity to now taking precautions to mitigate any future activity.

For Kate, it also changed how she dealt with the grief of her father's loss. "It's actually really interesting," Kate said. "My dad died suddenly in 2002 at fifty-four years old. Just dropped dead of a heart attack…. When he died, the little tiny bits of religious belief that I may have had left over from childhood went away completely. I said, 'Oh, he just went into the ground. He's just in the ground. Because if he could come back, he would contact me.'"

The weight of her grief dictated her feelings about what might happen after death. It was devastating to her that that person, that life, that force, just died and went into the ground and that was it. It changed her views, she said, on everything. Kate lost her connection to religion and the afterlife.

"I used to be really interested in ghosts growing up, but I stopped believing in it. So, when you came to investigate and gave answers, you have reaffirmed that there is an afterlife and people do go somewhere. Joe and I joke that we're going to haunt the Crocker Tavern House next, and we're going to sit on the front lawn and drink gin and yell to people as they pass by.

"Joking aside though, I actually do think that we go some-place afterwards and well, for my husband, it's to heaven," Kate explained. "I don't think that; that's not my personal belief. But I definitely want to mentally be where I am now because I've seen it. I've experienced this. I know what actually exists and I think knowledge is power."

Both Kate and Missy have used what were once terrifying experiences to better understand their own feelings on grief and mortality. Kate has been able to process the loss of her father in a different way. Before, she felt like there was nothing after death but now having had these experiences, she finds hope in the idea that we might be able to stick around. It changed her views on everything across the board: spirituality, religion, and the afterlife.

Missy sees Stephan and Emilia as friends and equals. It has made her more spiritual and she has found a different perspective regarding her Catholic upbringing. She was always taught that as a Catholic she would die and then go to heaven. However, her ghostly houseguests were devout Catholics, from the stories that she knows, and they are still around. Missy said, "It may not just be black and white, like you're here and you're gone. It's opened up a perspective on a whole different parallel space of what could be." She added, "I hope to God my mother comes and haunts me after she's gone."

CHAPTER 8

The Complicated Idea
of Crossing Over

Crossing over is a hotly debated topic in the paranormal community. Some believe that we, as living beings, can help guide spirits to the other side, and to find "the light." When I was first diving deep into the paranormal, I associated "crossing over" with a broader idea rather than an action.

I thought of crossing over as connecting to spirits, angels, or metaphysical forces—communicating directly to them or receiving information from them in a psychic manner. I loved the idea that someone could have this power and could relay information to those who needed it, like grieving loved ones looking for answers and hoping someone with a higher connection could provide relief from the trauma and sadness they were feeling. They, as psychics, would "cross over" from this life to the next and make contact with those on the other side.

Early in my metaphysical explorations, I followed meditations by psychic Lisa Williams to help find my own spirit guides. I thought that she was, in a way, helping me cross over—that from her coaching, I would be able to mentally explore a spiritual realm through meditation, and connect with my angels, ancestors, or guides.

Once, I had a deeply impactful experience doing one of her meditations. It involved imagining a staircase and walking to the top of it: when you opened the door, you would be in your own psychic realm, a version of your most idyllic surroundings. In this meditative world, you could explore your inner landscape and try to connect with your guardian angels.

I had done this a few times in the past, but on this occasion, it was different. I was in a strange waking sleep, but everything was clear and vivid. I was able to see who my angels were that guided me and kept me safe, something for only me to know. I lived for a few moments in this beautiful, peaceful, almost heavenly place. Then I was slowly drawn back into full consciousness, feeling refreshed and enlightened. I felt as if only a few minutes had passed, when in actuality forty-five minutes had flown by, essentially lost to time.

When I think about this experience, I truly feel that I was crossed over into the spirit realm. Looking back, it sounds a lot like self-hypnosis, but I don't care! I had a moment that made me feel like I had opened myself up to a world beyond my own. I crossed over into a space where I had a deepened spiritual connection, and brought lessons back with me into this reality. I came back with a newfound idea that I had not one, but two guardian angels. I believe they're familial ancestors, and that they will be with me throughout my life. There have been moments since then when I can actually acknowledge their intervention. That's the spiritual connection I associate with crossing over: making a connection to the other side that is otherworldly.

For me, crossing over has never had anything to do with helping a spirit to move on. It wasn't until I really got serious about paranormal investigation that I learned the more common interpretation among ghost hunters. People believe they can personally cross spirits into the next life, essentially forcing a spirit or ghost go to the light. When I first learned this, it seemed strange to me that a person would try to banish an entity out of our world and into the next without the spirit's consent, even if they were only trying to be helpful.

In total honesty, it still seems strange to me, but for different reasons. These days, I have more complicated feelings about crossing spirits over.

I believe in the power of intention, and that people can use their intention to manifest spiritual outcomes. If they truly believe they're crossing a ghost over, by all means, I can't take that away from them, but I personally don't believe it's possible to force a spirit to cross over.

As an investigator, you could use all the intention and manifestation you can muster to interact with a spirit, but it won't do any good for an entity who doesn't want to follow your line of thinking. Frankly, I find it a little rude to try to banish a spirit out of a space before they have the opportunity to communicate what they want or need, or explain their reason for staying behind in the first place. It's almost like you're assuming you know what's best for them without understanding anything about them.

Put yourself in their shoes. I imagine it like this: You pass away and then there is a period of time where you have to come to terms with what has happened. You have to figure out how to operate and exist in this new environment. You learn to communicate and interact with the living and the world around you. We don't know how long any of this takes—but what if someone realizes that you are a ghost in their space, and they immediately do something to cross you over? You don't get a chance to complete your afterlife goal. You didn't mean any harm and you have your own personal spiritual journey and business to attend to. What if that moment of crossing over resets all of the work that you have to do? The bottom line is no one knows what ghosts are going through on the other side, and we have to proceed with caution when it comes to interfering with those who have passed on.

Even though we provide closure or solutions for spirits that we help, it doesn't mean that the spirit is ready to leave this plane, or that the one thing we helped with was that spirit's only goal in the afterlife. A spirit can have multiple goals they want, or even need, to achieve before they move on to the next journey. Stephan and Emilia, the ghosts in Missy's house, were very vocal about protecting their home. Once communication between those two and Missy occurred, they began functioning as a team to restore the home, and the work even continues to this day. When the renovations are complete and Stephan and Emilia are satisfied, I think they will most likely cross over. But as of now, they have more work to do.

I've said it before, but it bears repeating: I believe in treating a ghost with as much respect, understanding, and empathy as I would any living person. Spirits were once people just like us, and I believe we should be using compassion to make a connection with them. If I were a ghost who hadn't fulfilled my spiritual mission, and someone came in and tried to usher me out of this world, I would: first, laugh in their face; second, get really angry and elevate all my ghostly activity to make it clear that I was pissed; and third, refuse to give the person who was attempting to do the crossing over the time of day ever again.

That's the way I see the situation with crossing spirits over. As investigators and psychics, we have the opportunity to truly understand their plight. It's a real privilege, not only for the sake of exploring the unknown and learning about what lies beyond our understanding, but to share those experiences and what we uncover with the world, so that everyone can better understand why ghosts exist. Trying to get rid of a ghost without listening to them is, to me, unfair treatment and an arrogant assumption. I absolutely understand the impulse to help. It's heartbreaking to hear a spirit in need of help, who's lost or doesn't know why they're still on the earthly plane, who is scared and alone. I don't understand the impulse to decide for them.

But that's assuming the act of "crossing someone over" through the power of your own will actually works. Amy and I have had cases in the past where we would hear that someone came in, "did a cleansing, and crossed the spirit over," only for us to find that the spirit is still there. In those instances, we've found the spirits to be unusually angry and aggressive, still trying to get a message across to the living.

I do, though, believe it's possible to help spirits cross over—by helping them find closure, so they feel as though their unfinished business is concluded. From my experience, listening to what a ghost has to say, trying to remedy the situation by what means you can, and sharing their message with the living is the best way for a spirit to cross over. Eventually, we find, they go wherever it is they want to go, on their own terms, only after they have been satisfied in this life. This is what we try to do when we are offering help to the dead. We provide support, help, or assistance, and then we let the entity decide what they want to do next.

It's a crossing over I can get behind. It's helping them achieve enough peace so that they decide they're ready to go.

It takes me back to that case with the spirit of Nancy. She said so clearly, "When we know, we'll go." That investigation was frustrating because it was so hard to figure out who and what was behind the activity. If Amy and I had gotten to the end of that case, and tried to get rid of her without truly listening to what she had to say, we would have never been gifted with such powerful statements. She imparted sentiments of love, the importance of living life to the fullest, and reassurance that peace will come once our time on this living plane is done. Not before then, but when the journey is complete.

I believe that Wilhelmina Crocker, when she said she was going home, was telling us that her journey was complete. She didn't mean she was going next door to her original family home—she was going "home" to her version of the afterlife. We didn't demand that of her, or cast her aside; we let her make that choice on her own.

Frankly, I would have loved to talk with her more about her current existence. If she had been willing, we could have found out much more information on what was currently happening to her spiritually, both why she didn't know she had died and why she was still around. But I didn't get the chance. Once she knew she had passed, it triggered her next step and she was gone. That to me is crossing over—offering help and then letting a spirit make their own choices. I've had people say that we are being heartless by not crossing over these spirits, who are mostly in pain and confused. I think what we are doing brings far more comfort for those who have unfinished business in the afterlife and supports a healthily transition. It's not demanding, it's understanding. It's compassion.

Crossing Over from a Psychic Perspective

Chip Coffey is a world-renowned psychic medium, and someone I trust when it comes to spirit communication. His abilities astound me time and time again, both when we're just together as friends and when he's investigating with us on *Kindred Spirits*. He helps people in deep and profound ways; sometimes his readings completely shock me, but in a positive sense.

"Helping a spirit to complete that transition between the world of the living and the realm of the dead—that's how I use the term crossing over," said Chip. But he would never presume to facilitate that crossing on his own volition. "That's not my job," he added. "It's not anybody's job.

Let's not get a big head and think that we are the ones who are going to fly in like Superman and save the day by sending these spirits across the great divide. I don't think that's the way it works."

To him, while we're alive, we can't know enough about death to really be able to process what it takes to cross over. "The way I look at it, we're souls in the flesh," Chip explained. "We may have lived many lifetimes, and we may have died many times, but somehow we've got amnesia about most of those other lifetimes and those experiences. So how are we, in the living world, going to guide somebody who is dead and trying to maneuver their way through this evolution? You can't do it because you don't know what's going on with that process."

Chip shared a story about how he had seen an attempt to cross a spirit over backfire in a spectacular way at a paranormal investigation event. "People had encountered a spirit and they felt like they needed to cross the spirit over," he said. The people there were *really* worked up about it, he said, fretting over *having* to cross the spirit over.

"At one point they asked, 'Do you need our help to cross over? We're going to help you cross over,'" Chip recalled. "The spirit on the recorder said, 'F*CK YOU.'" Clearly, that spirit wasn't interested in whatever those people thought they were going to do, no matter how good their intentions might have been.

To Chip, it boils down to a fundamental misunderstanding of what spirits are. He believes they exist in another realm, and can come visit if they choose to or they're asked to. "There are so many people that mistakenly assume that at a 'haunted' location, all those spirits there are earthbound, nomadic, trapped spirits," he said. "But they may very well be spirits that have finished that journey of crossing over and come back to visit or because we're conjuring them up."

We can't pretend that we completely understand the terms and conditions we have to face once we die. As an investigator, I've met many spirits at different stages. Some have come back just to check on things, while others are here and haven't made that final journey. We aren't the ones to tell them what to do or how to do it. We are merely observers of the unknown, documenting our experiences to better understand our own mortality and the hereafter.

Ghosts May Know More Than You Realize

Kathy Kelly is a paranormal researcher, lecturer, curator, and, in my opinion, one of the smartest people in our field of study. She witnessed a similar moment of a ghost asserting their own free will in the afterlife. Kathy was leading an investigation in an inn on the Jersey Shore, which had been experiencing phenomena for decades, but had lately been seeing more aggressive activity. "The busy season was longer than it had been in the past and the location was open during months that traditionally it had been closed and dormant," she explained. The owners were finding it difficult to use certain rooms, which were for staff and not for the public—those were the rooms the investigators focused their attention on.

"My protocol on an investigation is to not tell my team the stories or experiences of others until after they conclude their investigation reports," Kathy explained. "I do not want their experiences influenced by other people." Despite everyone going in cold and not getting any information beforehand, every investigator felt something uncomfortable and threatening in the suite of staff quarters.

There are some psychics who believe they personally, and not by divine intervention, can cross entities over who are still here. Kathy had a psychic medium at the inn as well, to aid in the investigation. "In this case, we had a very pervasive heaviness in the suite," she said. "After investigating for a few hours with several teams rotating through and getting the same results and feelings, we brought the medium in. She immediately connected with a male figure from the late 19th century. He was aggressive and angry and wanted everyone out of his space. There was a long backstory, but the gist of it was very unpleasant." Kathy revealed that he had been a bad and violent person in life, and was acting the same way in death.

Kathy explained that the medium tried to get him to leave, telling the man he could "move on" and "cross over." The simple response he gave was, "No." He refused because he had been raised Christian and had not lived a Christian life. In other words, he knew he was dead, he knew he could move on, and he refused to because he was afraid of the repercussions of his actions in life. "He believed that hell was waiting for him and nothing was going to move him," Kathy said. "In the end, we were able to confirm the experiences, but did very little to make the space more livable."

Is this spirit's fear of what awaited him on the other side concrete evidence that heaven or hell exists? No, but we do know for sure that the fear of what he believed was next made that spirit want to stay where he wanted to be, and nothing could be done to ease his fears or find solutions to stop the aggressive activity for the living. Sometimes, as investigators, we do all we can to fix a situation or make it better—but in the end, spirits have free will. If they don't want to cooperate, we can't force the issue.

But as someone who tries to help the living and the dead as my life's pursuit, that doesn't sit well with me. Isn't there anything to be done to help someone in that situation? "I tell people to pray for them," Chip said. "Ask their own spirit partners or their angels or whatever to come and help them through this process."

Chip has always been very vocal about his own spirit guides. He says these spirits, who are always with him, protect and guide him when he is receiving psychic information. "It's a conversation, like any conversation I have," he explained. "A client I am helping will say to me, 'My grandfather passed away recently. Can you help him to find his way across? Can you guide him in that process?' Then I ask my own family and people that I know, who have passed on, 'Is there something you can do? Maybe go find him and show him around.'" Chip's view is that the spirit can accept the offer of help and the friendly gesture, or not—it's their choice.

Sometimes, a spirit still isn't ready to accept that they've passed away. "There are some souls that are not ready to go yet," Chip said. "But there are also times when spirits have said, 'Pray for us,' when they've actually asked for our prayers."

But one thing is certain: It's not up to us to decide what those spirits need. "To feel like we have any right or responsibility to cross someone over when they haven't really asked for that just feels like if some stranger came up to me and said, 'You've gotta do this, or you need to do that.' Chances are I'm going to respond, 'Who are you? F*ck you!'"

The Idea of Crossing Over, and Coping with My Own Grief Over Lost Family Members

The one thing I think we can all agree on is that everyone eventually crosses over to somewhere: heaven, hell, purgatory, a ghostly state, a universal energy, nothingness—or infinite other possibilities. We all have to leave this world and this consciousness eventually. I sometimes think about those in my family who have already passed on and what their transitions were like. I have to assume that they all crossed over peacefully and have no unfinished business, because I've never heard from any of them. Well, let me qualify that: My Grannie has visited me in many dreams, but I will save that for another chapter.

I'm talking about seeing my family members, relatives, or even friends in the form of what we would categorize as paranormal evidence. You would think I'd have a direct line to those who have gone before me, but no, I've never had anyone I was close to come back to me and connect. Nor would I want them to, unless it was just to say hello.

Spirits who make contact usually want or need something—if someone I loved came to me, odds are, they'd need help, or have a message or mission. That would be okay, but what if I missed the signs that they were here? What then? Would they be stuck, trying to fulfill their mission and now trying to find someone else who can help them? I don't want to think about that.

I have my theories as to why my family hasn't reached out. Those in my family that I have lost have had great connection to their faith. They were in some ways always prepared, through scripture, to transition to the next life. They would be quick to relinquish their mortal ties for everlasting life.

Another thought is that those I have lost, say in the last ten years or so, not only know that I like to look for ghosts, but understand the reason why I look for ghosts. Maybe they don't want to get in the way and interrupt the work.

Or, simply put, maybe I don't want it, not even from a psychic point of view. I've had a lot of psychics come up to me who are very well meaning, and say, "I've just got to tell you something," or

"Someone is wanting me to tell you this or that." I cut them off before they can get any more words out. The bottom line is, I usually don't know this person, I don't know their abilities or how capable they are at receiving messages, and I have anxiety. What if they told me something that I didn't want to hear or wasn't ready to know? It could even be something that's not that intense, but that I might misinterpret as the worst thing ever. The same goes for psychics who watch us on television. I get messages warning me about this or that, based entirely on something they have just seen on an episode, even if that episode was from years ago. So, I don't like to be given unsolicited psychic advice.

I also rarely ask to be given a reading. The only time I can remember asking a psychic for intuition was from Chip. I have seen him change the lives of so many people on many occasions with the connections he makes. I trust him. That is the key takeaway from this. Trust.

My grannie had triple bypass surgery in October 2014, and, with her age and health, there was a chance she might not make it. The night before, I was at a big paranormal event in Minnesota. I had spoken with her on the phone and said my goodbyes in a way, just in case. I was trying to come to terms with what might be happening after I said I loved her and hung up the phone. I dried my eyes, pulled myself together, and headed down to the restaurant where a group of us were meeting for dinner.

Chip sat next to me, and I asked him if his spirit guides were telling him anything about the surgery. He said, "She's going to get through this surgery. She will make it through the surgery." He was right—she did make it through the surgery, and I got to spend another month talking with her on the phone, telling her I loved her, and feeling so thankful that she was in my life. However, an infection that she contracted after the surgery ultimately took her life. I asked Chip about this interaction recently and, as it turns out, he had been protecting me from what he knew was coming post-surgery. But I had only asked about the surgery itself, so he left it at that.

I've never asked Chip to reach out to anyone from my family or friends who have gone for a message or advice. My belief is that if they want to get in touch with me, they know where I am. Truly, I am not hiding from any spirits and I am with Chip often—if they needed to say something, they could go directly to the source, either me or him.

If there was anyone I would want to speak with, who has already crossed over—with Chip or any other psychic friend—it would be...oh, wait...I don't want to say it. If I do, then everyone will know and it wouldn't be real to me if or when it happens. So, I'll keep that to myself for now, and if it happens, I'll definitely let you know. Let's just say it would be a long time coming.

CHAPTER 9

The Light at the End of the Tunnel

The light at the end of the tunnel. We all have some understanding of what that phrase represents. It's the doorway to the eternal hereafter, a state that you journey through after you die and your essence/spirit/soul—however you prefer to think of it—leaves your physical body. It has been described, by those who have experienced the light and lived to tell the tale, with awe and love. People say they felt comforted and carried, with a new knowledge that once they pass on, they will enter their own version of eternity.

"Clear!" the doctor yells, preparing the defibrillator. Using two paddles, pulsing with electricity, they place them on your chest. The doctor administers one shock after another to jumpstart your heart. Meanwhile, you are inching closer and closer to that breathtaking light. You may enter into a world of beauty and familiarity, seeing family and loved ones who have gone before. There is a sense of peace and calm that is nothing like you have ever known.

"Clear!" Another shock. Suddenly the pull you feel is reversing. No longer are you flying toward your great beyond, but are now being tugged back to your mortal vessel. It isn't your time to go. Just as quickly as you left your flesh and blood, you are back—but now, you're faced with the reality of your experience.

What I have just described is similar to what most people describe when they discuss having had a near-death experience, or NDE. The common theme seems be a journey to somewhere with a light at the end. There are also more complicated accounts of NDEs where a person can see themselves lying in the hospital bed while they are floating over their body, with a bird's eye view of what's happening. Some have angels or other beings escort them through the tunnel, guiding them to the point when they discover it isn't their time to leave the earth and must return to this realm.

"Near death" implies that you get very close to the line of something irreversible, and come back from it. The overall consensus is that once you cross a certain point, whether it be a threshold, circle of light, river, or other boundary, there is absolutely no going back. Some say they were able to make a choice, asking or opting to return, while others were told it simply wasn't their time. Whatever the experience, it's powerful.

I've always thought about near-death experiences as a way to show the rest of us that "something" happens once we die. They're not telling us where we go, but they *are* showing us how we get there, and that's a huge step toward the path of discovery.

Researchers have discovered that the brain still operates for a period of time after death. "As the heart stops and we die, the brain is flatlined and nonfunctional," Sam Parnia, MD, PhD, said in an interview with Neo.Life. "However, using brain electrical monitoring, there is growing evidence that in this state (as people pass away), there are markers of activity (beta, delta, and sometimes gamma waves) that emerge for a very short period. These are ordinarily found when people are having conscious experiences, but now they are also seen to emerge at the time of death, when the rest of the brain has a background of being flat."

A preeminent researcher in near-death brain function and resuscitation, Dr. Parnia is the Director of Critical Care and Resuscitation Research at NYU Langone Health, and has written extensively about near-death experiences—which he prefers to call "actual death experiences."

"As people die and the parts of the brain that are ordinarily active during our day-to-day lives are no longer required and shut down, they enable the disinhibition of areas in the brain that are otherwise ordinarily not active and are inhibited in day-to-day life," he continued. "This is what we are seeing with the emergence of those brain markers at the time of death. This disinhibition of these areas then seems to give people access to dimensions of reality that they would ordinarily not have access to in day-to-day life. This may be important from an evolutionary perspective, as they may not be needed until we reach death."

Dr. Parnia is suggesting that during a near-death experience, we tap into areas of our brain that allow us the ability to "see" beyond our normal capabilities. We are harnessing powers of our brain that are normally dormant or inaccessible. "It is not so much that the brain is creating these experiences as a hallucination or illusion," he said, "but rather the brain is enabling access to aspects of reality and a person's own consciousness." Take a minute to imagine the possibilities of the untapped parts of our brain. Could it be that we *all* have a psychic sense, or the ability to perceive other dimensions, and those capabilities are just locked in unused parts of our brain?

Accessing those other parts of the brain might just explain how psychics tap into their abilities. And, as Dr. Parnia points out, that ability might be significant with regard to evolution. There have always been psychics and mediums, but it seems to me like they are more prevalent and respected now than ever before. What if we, as a species, are beginning to gain access to these parts of our brains even before we reach death?

What I love about Dr. Parnia's study is that he is acknowledging that the brain accesses a different function when we are experiencing death, and continues to perform tasks. We always talk about death being a journey to somewhere else. What if this is the way our journey begins? Our brain taps into a new way of operation and jumpstarts our next chapter into the afterlife. After all, spirits that we communicate with on the other side act the same as we do. They are functioning, at least cognitively, the same way as the living.

A lot of people who survive a near-death experience talk about "seeing their life flash before their eyes." They take the measure of their time on Earth; many report feeling judgment, not from a divine being, but from themselves. They reflect on what they feel they could have done better, or how they were perceived by the people in their lives.

Dr. Parnia brought up this major theme as a lucid experience that is unique to each individual at the edge of death. He also pointed out a fascinating aspect of the experience, that the encounter people report having is often at odds with what they've been taught to expect at the moment of death, or what their belief system dictates *should* happen at that time.

"People do not experience [exactly] what their religions had taught them, and atheists and agnostics also experience the same review of their lives and lucidity with death," Dr. Parnia said. "So, in short, this experience and what science is discovering at the time of death seems to transcend any specific religious doctrine." It makes sense: we can believe whatever we want to believe to help support our choices in life and the way we want to live spiritually, but in the end, we are all the same. We are all living a human existence under different circumstances and are all connected by the singular commonality of death. Part of me wonders whether there is a universal answer to what comes next, and that people collectively access it, in spite of their personal doctrines, which is why they report experiencing fundamentally the same thing.

A First-Hand Account of a Near-Death Experience

My dear friend and fellow paranormal investigator John E.L. Tenney has been on *Kindred Spirits* many times, including a case in which the homeowner had had an NDE. John has also experienced, and come back from, his own near-death experience. I can't think of a better person to help describe what it's like.

"The most common near-death experience is a tunnel of light," he told me. "Loved ones going to a better place. And that is very easy to discuss because it is describable. There is a white light, there is a tunnel, there is movement, there is emotion, there are things to talk about. And it's pleasant." John has been actively involved in the field of anomalistic, conspiratorial, occult, ufological, and paranormal research for well over three decades (say that five times fast!). "And people are very willing to discuss those experiences."

I usually refer to John as the most interesting man in the paranormal world. His stories captivate, and he can always be seen outside events and conventions with a gathering of very eager listeners, catching the craziest story ever told.

"The second most common near-death experience is just an out-of-body experience," he continued. "People see themselves on the roof of the ambulance. They see themselves being operated on. They see the doctors trying to bring them back to life. And they can see their physical body because they are outside of their physical body."

When he was eighteen, John had a heart attack, and he was clinically dead for three-and-a-half minutes. But his experience didn't look anything like those two other types.

"The uncommonly spoken about near-death experience is mine, because it lacks descriptors, it lacks good language to describe a purely infinite consciousness experience," he said. "My death experience is difficult to discuss because where most people have an experience that contains objects and people and places and feelings, my death experience was one of void. It was one of infinity, emptiness, and nothingness."

This depiction of eternity seems terrifying, almost like you are being buried alive in a place with dark—darker than dark—surroundings of pure emptiness. "And since there is nothing there," he said, then paused, processing what had occurred to him so many years ago, frame by frame, "to say that it's even nothing seems incorrect to me, because nothing is something. I went from our world to a world where everything was only me. Only I existed. I had only ever existed, forever. Everything has always only been me. When I first had that realization, with what I would call 'a memory of being alive,' my first reaction was to call out to someone. That moment lasts forever because there's no time there. So, for an infinite amount of time, I had been screaming out for there to be something other than me in a void, which had only ever been me. There was no one to call out to and I had been there forever trying to call out to someone."

So many thoughts popped into my head as he was talking. I thought about the expanse of the universe, the nothingness of the mind, the general idea that matter never being destroyed or created must exist somewhere at all times. John was screaming into the vastness of space, void of light and stars, and was everything and everywhere all at once and nowhere at the same time.

Even though John was experiencing a feeling of forever, he had only been physically dead for a short period. "I was dead [in this world] for three and a half minutes," he explained. "For me, I was dead for forever. Which means that talking to you now, I'm talking to you from a place which is 'after forever,' which in our minds is impossible."

Eternal life comes up quite a bit in religious conversations and also when thinking of our existence in the afterlife. Heaven, or some world similar, is a place where we go to "live" for eternity. John believes his version of eternity was shaped by his own spiritual beliefs, or lack thereof, at the time. "I was lost," he said of his former state of spiritual health. "I didn't have a spiritual belief system, and I really only believed in myself. When I died, I got a feeling of isolation, aloneness, and only myself in that void." A ghost in our world may eventually end up getting to their personal place of forever. Possibly, they are already in their forever state when we are speaking with them during investigations. In his near-death experience, John encountered what he says is the "idea" of forever; that the world that we exist in, like where you are right now reading this book, is a blip in that forever.

He compared it to a dream. When you are asleep, there is this time where you are witnessing tangible and sometimes intense interactions. Then you wake up, and you're back in the real world. "If you use this analogy and you apply it to the whole idea that you exist forever before you are born," John said, "then there's a little blip of time where you're alive and you experience emotions, feelings, colors, and beings. Then you die and you go back to forever. Being an inhuman body [in forever] is more like being in a dream than it is like being awake."

John seemingly has, by his account, already experienced forever and now he's back—almost as if he was reincarnated back into this world, but kept his former vessel. He died, and became what he always was and what he always will be, and now he's back experiencing another blip. John's perspective shifted after his NDE. "It shaped and changed me as a transformational experience into someone looking deeper into spiritual qualities and spiritual beliefs, and not solely relying on myself for the answers."

In that three and a half Earth minutes while he was dead, where was everyone else? "I think that when I died and thought that I was alone, it was because I had never experienced, outside of my family, any close relationships with anyone," he said. "When you have a close relationship with someone, you are *one* with that person." John said that he was screaming out for others, but how did he know there were even others to connect with? In most NDE experiences, people have visions of other people, or divine beings. John had a nothingness, but in that blank space, did he somehow know that there were others in the darkness?

"Since I am everything forever and everywhere and anything, that means that I was also 'you,'" he explained. "So, when I say alone, what I'm saying is I was the amalgamation of every single person that has ever existed. That ever will exist. That has ever been born, lived, and died. That ever will be born, live, and die."

But in that all-encompassing state, John discovered, he had power and agency. "Since I was everything, I was also able to return myself back to this reality," John said. "There's no good way to explain, because there were no emotions there. There were simply ideas. And it's not as if my real-world consciousness reached into that void and it was *me* in that realm, making the decision to come back. So, in the midst of being the idea of reaching out to others, I also became an idea, which was: Do I want this specific forever to persist forever? And when I became that idea, there was a moment when I then became the idea of wanting more than forever, more than infinite aloneness. And, as soon as I became that idea of not wanting infinite aloneness, I opened my eyes in the hospital and was alive. I didn't want to be alone. I wanted more than just me. In our world, [the decision] was a fraction of a second. But then, in that world, [the decision] could have taken forever, billions of years."

John's views on his own spirituality have changed over the years. He believes that when he journeys to the afterlife once more, his experience will be similar but more connected. He feels that void that he experienced is only a transitional state and there will be something after, just as he returned back to this life after his NDE. "As my relationships with people grow, in this life, and as I make more formative and inclusive bonds, I realize all of my friends and family are one. So when I die, I will be that one again, but I'll be everybody's one. That's not scary or intimidating to me at all. That's actually kind of beautiful. It's the perfect coalescence of relationships."

The hard thing to grapple with is how we can continue to live this life to the fullest if we believe unconditionally that there is life, or rebirth, in the next. On the one hand, I have always been taught about an afterlife where all of our friends and loved ones will be together again, and I really connect with that. However, I think there's a danger that having that belief could make us lose sight of what is important in the earthly here and now. If we know without a doubt and with pure confidence that we will see each other again one day, and that we will have the ability to continue to live our afterlives in the same way we always have, we could take for granted what we have in this existence while focusing on the next. If we had absolute knowledge, we'd start to view life in very different ways.

Maybe we'd have a flippancy about death that would promote unhealthy habits and experiences.

But maybe we can find a balance from these near-death experiences. "I couldn't understand what had happened to me and why it would happen to me," John said. "It was a very negative experience for me for the first year. It wasn't until I realized how much more I appreciated everything that I started to understand what a positive experience it had been—how much more I appreciated things like the color brown, or how much I appreciated having my heart broken and crying. I was in a place [in the afterlife], or seemed to be in a place, where I would have no longer felt love. I would've no longer felt hate. I would've no longer felt jealousy. I would've no longer felt anything because there was nothing there. And I had been returned to this place full of colors and sights and sounds and emotions and feelings with a new appreciation of how wonderful it is to be able to experience them in body because there will come a time when I won't be able to experience them in body."

I've heard that same lesson from spirits who have unfinished business or who want to remind us to live our lives to the fullest, like Nancy appreciating her birds and savoring all the love she had in life. John's experience was a test of his own beliefs, and he is still learning from that experience to this day. In everything he does, he remembers what that moment was like, and it helps him stop and appreciate what is here and now. The Bible says that heaven is a place with no worry or grief. That we have no struggles or sickness, and there will never be death. In a way, John's experience lines up with that teaching because where he was, there was no emotion or feeling at all. It was a vast void where we are everything, everywhere, and everyone all at once into infinity.

Applying the Lessons of NDEs to This Existence

Sometimes after a near-death experience, people say they have changed more than just their outlook on their own human existence. Some find that they are so spiritually changed that they are still connected to the other side and can access that world psychically. But having an NDE isn't the only way to do that. There are a number of ways, in my opinion, for us to connect to the spirit realm without having a near-death experience.

Meditation is a way to slow down and connect to the energy and world around you. Thoughts flow in and out and, every once in a while, you may have a strong premonition or a moment of pure connection to someone you have lost. I find that when I "drop in" and focus a bit more in an investigation, really connecting my inner feelings to the questions we are asking of the spirits, I tend to get more responses. I see it as tapping into that psychic part of the brain that I think everyone could access if they tried.

Earlier I posited that maybe psychics could have the ability to access those sections of our brain that remain dormant until we die. This is a strong argument for that theory. There have been people who have had near-death experiences and find that the little part of their brain once closed to psychic abilities is unlocked and fully open. It doesn't shut off after the experience ends, but enhances the world around them for the rest of their time on this side of the veil. Others seem to be more open and connected to the physical and spiritual world around them. John calls it "residue."

"The thing that's interesting to me as a researcher of paranormal phenomena," said John, "is that since my death experience, I have noticed that whatever you want to call them—ghosts or spirits or apparitions—how they deal with me has changed. It seems to me that they know I have been to a place similar to where they are now.

I have had a number of experiences where it seems to be upsetting to them that I was allowed to return back to the living. For other entities, they seem to be extremely happy that they have someone who can match the experience they're currently having."

If John does have an edge in communication with the dead, it would explain so much. He has a truly unique approach to investigating the paranormal, using his extensive knowledge combined with life experience to help explain and explore all kinds of paranormal activity. We have done a number of cases together, and he's usually the most level-headed person in the room. He uses the veritable encyclopedia of information in his head, and it supports our work and cases with new ideas from countless perspectives.

Since the time of his near-death experience, John has dedicated his life to the field of supernatural study, not only with ghosts, but with cryptids, UFOs, and other topics of high strangeness. It seems as if his destiny was to do what he is doing at this very moment in time. Similar to John, I always felt that was why I find myself where I am today, in this career, even writing this book. The subject chose me, not the other way around. I didn't have a choice in the matter.

But does John have a stronger connection to the other side than most because of his experience? How does he use this to his advantage? After all, he has turned that initial trauma into a positive thing. "Well, I don't talk about this a lot," John paused briefly, choosing his words carefully. "When I'm doing investigations, when I'm trying to interact with denizens who may not exist in this reality, a lot of the time I'm really focusing my concentration on speaking to them via [the version of] myself who is dead in the future."

Since he believes, from his experience, everything is everything, he can harness that idea to tap into deeper communication. "In the future I know that this body's not going to exist anymore, but 'John' will still exist in some state," he said. "The easiest way for me to make contact with spirits that don't exist in bodily form in this reality, which I learned from being in a near-death experience, is a very simple lesson: I can communicate better with people or beings or energies that aren't in this reality by learning to better communicate effectively with people who exist in my reality with me. The better I am with communicating with other humans, the better I am as a communicator with those who were human at one time."

Like John, I have always tried to carry myself in a certain way when dealing with others. Maybe it was my upbringing with saying "ma'am" and "sir," but I feel it's very important to show others respect and try to have common sense when it comes to interacting with the living. It is hard, believe me, and I don't get it right all the time. However, when I meet people for the first time, it is so much better to greet them with a smile and a handshake, and to make sure we level the playing field. I am no better than anyone else and no one is better than me. We are all the same in the eyes of the universe.

Having that outlook on life does indeed make me have a more sympathetic view of the afterlife. If you are trying to heighten your psychic sensitivity or make contact with the other side, use this idea as a guide to see if you can better your results. If you aren't investigating for ghosts this can even help you in the day-to-day world—though you may already be communicating with spirits without even knowing it.

"The most common form of spirit communication that's practiced across the world is prayer," John said. "People knowingly, with full belief, understand that when they close their eyes and they speak silently in their mind, that their thoughts are discerned at a distance by another intelligence." No wonder spirits ask for prayer. Not only is it universal, but it can be done by anyone, not just paranormal investigators. Maybe some spirits don't even realize we travel the world looking for entities like them all the time, but rather just recognize that we are fellow humans and we can offer them comfort or support in the form of prayer communication.

I tend to drop in a bit deeper when I am investigating. I grew up in the church so I learned how to pray, and though I now pray in my own particular way, I have come to realize that I harness a prayerful intention when speaking to the non-living. While I may not start the conversation with "Dear God," I have the same reverence and openness when I say, "If there is anyone here with us, please reach out." It's a form of spiritual connection, an energetic cord from the living to the dead, providing a way to help and nurture someone who has passed on. I think Amy and I really feel it when we are in that spiritual zone. We start to get more answers on our recorders, and our investigative equipment is activated more frequently. It comes with a feeling that we are one with our surroundings. Everything is truly everything.

John had a traumatic experience, but I think he's lucky to have the unique insight and perspective that came from it. He can tell us these stories and we can understand every word, but we won't ever be able to truly grasp the feeling. When he talks about that moment and what he has learned from it, it's easy to tell that there is so much more than mere words going on. It's a physical and spiritual awakening that is singular and specific to him and him alone.

"I think that my experience was completely transformational in the sense that the person I am today is so far beyond where I think I would have been if the experience didn't happen," John explained. "I don't think that I would be alive right now had I not died, which sounds really weird. But I think that dying not only gave me a greater appreciation for life, but also that dying extended my bodily life. I feel like—again, this is purely from my perspective—I feel like the universe and the cosmos, God, whatever you want call it, I feel like it gave me what I needed for me to make a fully informed decision as to what I wanted next."

I believe, on some level, that everything happens for a reason. A world without John, his friendship, or his knowledge would not be a world I would have wanted either. I needed to know, so I asked him, now that he's died once and had such an intense experience, would he choose to be a ghost, if he could, for his next death experience? "No," he said, without any hesitation. "Because I feel like, solely through my perspective, this planet and all of the things on it and all of the people are created for someone [with a] body. Colors, sight, sound, smells, emotions are made for someone in a physical body. For me to stay here and not be able to see with human eyes and hear with human ears, I wouldn't want to experience this world in that way."

Well, if he's not going to stick around this plane, what does the idea of the afterlife look like for him now? "It's funny because, if you had asked me when I was eighteen, I would have told you it would look exactly like the opposite of my experience that I had," John said. "I told you that my experience was hellish and that I thought I was in hell. Now, thirty some odd years later, I would tell you that my heaven looks like my experience when I was eighteen: that I would be a conglomeration, that I would be at one with everyone and everything in the universe. That I would be able to explore the infinity and the foreverness of everything with everyone else. That seems like heaven to me."

It's definitely not a bad version of the hereafter. It has a human experience that both the living and the dead are always looking for: connection. There is a peace to his version, and it's based on experience. I wouldn't mind being able to mesh with the entire world around me and expand beyond the boundaries of time and space. Until, that is, we get to the end of forever and possibly come back?

From John's point of view, he's literally on the other side of forever. He's after eternity, and what he knows and feels now is an expansion of his former self he left behind at eighteen years old. Those who have had a near-death experience are all in their own specific "after eternity," and are infinitely different from those that have not had that experience. What if we could have a death experience, to better connect with those in the afterlife, but without the actual death part? It turns out, I got to experience that myself.

Piercing the Veil with an Unusual Investigative Technique

When your friend whom you trust and respect, says, "Here, drink this haunted honey," you might hesitate, but I didn't. Okay, maybe I did a little—but Greg Newkirk is pretty convincing.

On season six of *Kindred Spirits*, Amy and I were investigating Liberty Hall in Union, New Jersey. The property was built in 1772, and the original Kean family lived there for generations until it became a museum in 1995. The paranormal activity that people who worked at the museum normally experienced had picked up a bit and started to become aggressive, and the staff wanted to find out if any Keans were still around and in need of something.

Through our investigation, we felt fairly convinced that Captain John Kean was still in Liberty Hall in spirit form and was upset. We didn't know why and we couldn't get the answer from him. So, Greg came up with a plan and gave us a few tools to help one of us become a bit more connected with the spirits in the home.

"There's a small ritual that involves the ingestion of a very special type of honey," he explained on the episode. "The honey was harvested by bees in a gigantic cemetery in England. So, [when you eat the honey] you are in a way communing with the dead, and then you can spend a few minutes meditating on death and what it's like to be a ghost. While that honey is in your system, you will be a little bit closer."

Yep, just some normal honey. I was ready for the journey.

Using meditation to drop in to a more spiritual place isn't a foreign idea to me. I slow down my breathing, cultivate a stillness in body and mind, and enter into a place where I can more deeply explore my interior landscape. There are many ways to prepare to meditate. Some people play music or use singing bowls. Others use herbs, incense, and oils. They're all tools to help a person center and focus on what they would like to achieve personally and spiritually during the journey.

For this honey experiment, the idea was to connect to the dead in a way that was much more intimate than a normal meditative state. All of the tools and preparation for it focused on death, the idea of the afterlife, and the hope that we would gain answers.

We made our way into the parlor of this gigantic mansion. Most of those who had lived in Liberty Hall, and passed away over the years, had their wakes held in the parlor of the home, including the person we wanted to contact the most.

In trying to open myself up to an experience like this, I had to consciously remove the guards I had naturally built up. I asked my guardian angels to step aside, and tried to fully trust the process. It was an exploration of massive proportions, and I wanted to be ready to receive the answers that I was seeking. I was open, vulnerable, receptive, and anxious. I didn't think I would actually die, but what if I saw or experienced something so terrifying—like John did—that I didn't want to look for ghosts anymore?

For me, the risk didn't outweigh the experience. I took the small vial of honey, held it to my lips, and drank with the reverence appropriate for this ritual. Some viewers speculated that there was a psychedelic substance in the honey, but it was just honey, plain and simple. Well, honey made by bees who harvest their nectar from flowers growing out of the graves of the dead. Psychedelic, no. Mind-altering, maybe.

To prepare for the journey, I focused on the idea that the honey came from the dead. I visualized infusing myself into the sweet golden syrup, and imagined being one with everyone and everything in the afterlife. I laid on the floor in the spot that seemed most appropriate for a coffin to be during a wake.

Greg showed me a small carved figure that was half human and half jackal: Anubis, the Egyptian guardian of the dead, god of funerary rites, protector of graves, and guide to the underworld. I took the idol from Greg; while it wasn't heavy, it seemed to hold massive weight and fit into the palm of my hand as if it had always been there. They covered me with a burial shroud. Placing one large coin on each of my eyelids, Greg said, "Coins to pay the ferryman."

"While you're laying here by yourself, meditate on the idea of death and the particular frustrations that you have felt trying to communicate with the other side," Greg said. "When you feel like you've made a connection, you can pull the shroud off. And that is your symbolic rebirth into the spirit world. Rest in peace, Adam." With that final farewell, Amy and Greg left me alone in the space to travel through the underworld.

I asked him recently how he came up with such an experiment. "Every single element of that ritual had a point," he said. "It was symbolic of a connection to the underworld. When I was in England, we went on a tour of Highgate Cemetery and as we were there, I noticed that they had beehives everywhere. I thought it was such a cool thing. When we went to the gift shop later, I saw they actually sold honey from the beehives that they kept in the cemetery. That was the first inkling of that ritual. There's life teeming above the surface that is being fed by the dead below. What could make you more in touch with a haunted space than eating the honey that has been made by the decay of the dead?"

Laying there with coins over my eyes and the shroud over my head, it was hard to shake the feeling of claustrophobia and entrapment. Anxiety started to get the best of me. I focused on my breath. *Inhale in and exhale out.* I started to drop a bit deeper into the meditation with each separate breath. The best way to describe "dropping in" as I experience it is to picture yourself falling through space—and as I fell deeper into whatever this void was, the sounds of the environment around me slowly began to dissolve into silence. I was no longer listening with my ears but with my whole self. I couldn't see, but I felt like my body was connected to my environment more than it had ever been.

I followed Greg's instructions and started thinking about the difficulties that we have as investigators in communicating with the dead. Sometimes I feel like spirits can't understand the living, as if we are speaking two different languages. As an investigator, I don't ever really know who I am specifically talking to on the other side until it is confirmed by the entity, and the fear of asking the wrong question is always in the back of my mind.

As these thoughts rushed in, I slowly became aware of the answers to my frustrations. They mirrored each other. As much as I sometimes feel frustrated by not being heard by those I am trying to communicate with in the afterlife, those who have passed on struggle even more to communicate with the living. I got an overwhelming urge to scream out to get someone, anyone's attention, so that I, as dead, would be acknowledged and recognized.

That feeling is similar to what John described in his near-death experience. I felt that if someone had just said my name, the anxiety and overwhelming sense of loss that I was feeling would go away. I knew that Greg and Amy were in the building, monitoring my progress, and I kept thinking over and over if one of them would just say my name, if a crew member even would just say my name, if someone would come into the room and say, "Adam? Are you okay?," then I could acknowledge that I was all right and we could continue with the experiment.

The deep longing to be acknowledged was extremely heavy and full of desperation. I think this feeling might be tied to why spirits who aren't malevolent sometimes scratch people. The emotional weight of the experience has to be intense, especially if it's anything like what I was going through. At one point I thought I heard Amy walk into the room, because I could hear the creaking of wooden floors near the entrance to the parlor. I swore she came halfway into the room, checked visually see how I was doing, and then walked out. She didn't say my name and she didn't ask if I was okay, but I swore that she was there for a brief moment. I knew she was, so much so that I started to repeat: "Say my name. Just say my name. Say my name. Ask me if I'm okay. Say Adam."

Months later, I was telling this story to a crowd of people and Amy interrupted. "I'm sorry, I just have to stop you for a second," she said. "I've heard you say this story about someone coming to check on you, but no one walked into that room at all, Adam. You were alone the entire time."

So, what was that? Who checked on me? Maybe I finally became aware of the spirits that were in the space with me? Because, soon after the moment I thought Amy checked on me, I got a strong visual of many people standing around my body, looking down on me as I lay on the floor in the parlor. I was in a dreamlike state but it was so vivid. I can see it now as I think about it; these people seemed ethereal and translucent, but alive. Even though I couldn't make out physical features or what they were wearing, I just knew their appearances were otherworldly and their clothing had a historic nature. They were not people from my time, but from a time that had already passed—many times that have already passed.

At this point, my body felt like it weighed a thousand tons. I was sinking into the floor, and strangely enough found comfort in the quiet coziness of my situation. My anxiety was gone and I knew that I wasn't alone, yet I still needed the acknowledgment. Then, in the silence of my lonely thought, one spirit spoke to me out of all those who were standing around me, and confirmed that what I was feeling was exactly what they were feeling. Not with actual words, but as if to implant the entire idea all at once, communicating for everyone there. They wanted acknowledgment, communication, understanding, respect—and if one living person would only say their name, they would once again find peace, but only for a period of time.

I don't know how I knew specifically that is what they wanted, but without a doubt in my mind, that's what I was shown during that experience. After a few more moments, I was ready to return to the living realm. I took one last deep breath, and with what felt like all the strength I could muster, I reached my right arm over my body and slowly pulled back the burial shroud. Another deep inhalation, and I sat up, allowing the coins to fall from my eyes. Amy said I looked like a zombie coming back to life, and I felt that way (except for the urge to eat brains, thankfully). Slowly opening my eyes to the world around me and coming back into focus, I felt that "residue" that John talks about. Something had changed for me, and that residue was lingering; I felt more connected and more able to communicate with spirits in that location than I had ever felt in my life.

The feeling and experience didn't go to waste. We used it to propel the rest of that investigation. I strongly believe that it helped us get major responses to our questions, and we were able to finally get answers for those who worked at Liberty Hall. Whether it was the actual experiment or whether I proved to the spirits that I was willing to go to great lengths to help them, it worked; something worked. We were able to help in the end.

To this day, I still feel connected to that moment. When I investigate now and I drop into the idea of deeper communication in a prayer-like state, I think there's a small part of me that those spirits recognize as themselves. In the way that John feels like he is accessing his own experience, which was far greater than the one I had, in some small way I might be changed as well. If we are all connected and everything is everything all at once, then there is no doubt in my mind, as living human beings, we can tap in to that spiritual place and create deeper connections with the afterlife.

PART THREE

How the Paranormal Helps Us Cope with Death and Knowing (or Not Knowing) What's Next

CHAPTER 10

See You in My Dreams

"To die, to sleep;
To sleep: perchance to dream: ay, there's the rub;
For in that sleep of death what dreams may come
When we have shuffled off this mortal coil,
Must give us pause—"

—WILLIAM SHAKESPEARE, *HAMLET*

That might be the most beautiful way anyone has speculated about the afterlife. "What dreams may come / When we have shuffled off this mortal coil," gives me such a sense of wonder and intrigue. I imagine that, just as with the dreams we have while alive, the possibilities are limitless. We die, but then we experience a whole new level of consciousness. Does it feel like a dream state all the time? Is the next phase of existence a waking dream?

Those who have had near-death experiences often describe their level of consciousness as being in a "dreamlike state," and during the haunted honey experiment, it felt like I was having the most vivid

147

dream imaginable, which I still think about to this day. Dreaming is so powerful, especially when connecting to your higher mind or to a different phase of existence. In that place we go while sleeping, we have access to a different level of thoughts, memories, and emotions. Some experiences feel so real we wake up with the residue of the emotions we felt, and carry those into our waking days.

Comparing death to a dream state has been happening throughout history, all over the world. "Although these cultures [Australia, South Pacific, Africa, China, India, Egypt, Greece, etc.] have very different philosophical and spiritual worldviews, they share a fundamental belief that when we sleep, a part of ourselves (soul, spirit, ethereal self, etc.) is free to perceive other realities, travel to other-worldly realms, and gain important knowledge and wisdom," wrote Kelly Bulkeley, Ph.D., and Reverend Patricia Bulkley in their book *Dreaming Beyond Death.* "Death, in this perspective, is the final and permanent release of that part of ourselves, a sleep from which one never awakens, a dream that never ends."

Even from a biblical perspective the concept of sleep as death is strong. Matt Arnold, in his *Premier Christianity* article "Ghosts, haunted houses and bumps in the night: What the Bible really says about all things spooky," pointed to places in the Bible where scripture uses the metaphor of sleep as death. In particular, he highlighted 1 Thessalonians 4:13–14, which reads, "But we do not want you to be uninformed, brothers, about those who are asleep, that you may not grieve as others do who have no hope. For since we believe that Jesus died and rose again, even so, through Jesus, God will bring with him those who have fallen asleep."

"Some claim this shows the dead are inactive," Matt wrote. "However, this ignores the power of the metaphor. Sleepers still exist in the same way that someone in the grave still exists; they have a state of awareness, but one that the awake are unable to access. Modern technology reveals our brain's incredible activity, even while asleep. Rather than unconscious existence, this metaphor opens the idea that the dead are conscious in a way that was not obvious to previous generations."

I think that the comparison of dream and death, and death as sleep, is so universal and ancient because the vast majority of us have dreams. Just as people have different views of what the afterlife looks like, we also experience dreams in immeasurable variety. My dreams are in vivid color, while I know that some people dream in black and white. I have had dreams so real and palpable that I wake up in an emotional state that's hard to shake. Through bad dreams, good dreams, adventurous dreams, dreams that deal with love and relationships, and dreams that deal with death, the common thread is that the experiences we have inside them are limitless.

In the same way that ghosts have agency in the afterlife, I have experienced lucid dreams in which I've had active awareness. I knew I was dreaming, and I was able to make my own decisions and stop myself from doing something that would immediately turn the experience into a bad dream. I was able to be the orchestrator of an otherworldly experience. In my most incredible and real lucid dream moments, I've dreamed of someone who has passed on, and I have been able to interact with them as though they are still alive.

Spiritual visitations in dreams are very rare. According to *Dreaming Beyond Death*, they account for perhaps 1 percent of all dreams. I think of it like winning the dream lottery: it's extremely real, even though we know we are dreaming, and often the experience provides some sort of information or knowledge we had not known before. We can learn things from those who are with us in the dream, but not with us in our mortal realm. If a loved one visits us, we can interact with them again as if they are alive; we can touch them, talk to them, feel their entire presence.

The authors of *Dreaming Beyond Death* refer to visitation dreams as, "Striking, emotionally intense dreams in which a recently deceased loved one returns to provide guidance, reassurance, and/or warning."

"What makes visitation dreams so memorable is an unusual intensity and vividness that sharply distinguishes them from the majority of other dreaming experiences," they write. "People often speak of a visitation dream as feeling 'realer than real,' and when the dreamers awaken these electrifying feelings carry over into waking awareness, remaining surprisingly strong and easy to recollect many years later."

According to their logic, these dreams are proof that ghosts still have emotions and prize the relationships they had in life. They write, "Visitation dreams do not deny death so much as transcend it, providing experiential evidence of human connections that extend beyond the end of mortal life."

Having had my own ghostly dreams, I know they're very personal and private and truly hard to forget. The life-affirming nature of moments like that stick with you long after anything else. But I'm still not sure if they're paranormal in nature, or a moment of divine intervention. Maybe both?

Amy Bruni has also experienced a visitation dream, one that many years later is still deeply emotionally impactful for her.

"My grandpa died very suddenly and unexpectedly at age seventy of a heart aneurysm," she told me. "He was supposed to come to my house that day for a barbecue, and he sent me an email saying he really didn't feel well and that my grandma was taking him to the hospital. My family is notoriously flaky, so I thought it was just an excuse and I remember being angry and not even answering. Later that day, while the rest of my family was together at the barbecue, we got the call that my grandpa did not make it. I carried that guilt with me in my soul—that he was so unwell and took the time to write me an email and I hadn't even bothered to respond."

Amy's grandfather loved tennis so much that he played it to the very day he died. He actually fell ill playing tennis that day, and that's why he needed to go to the hospital. A few weeks before that, she had taken him to see his favorite tennis player, Andre Agassi. "As we were cruising to the tennis match, he put a CD in his CD player and said, 'Do you like Ah-ba?'" she recalled. "And I said, 'ABBA?' And he responded, 'Yes, Ah-ba.' I giggled as we cruised with the windows down, listening to 'Dancing Queen.'"

After he died, Amy had a dream about him. "My grandpa and I were cruising in his car, windows down, chatting and listening to ABBA," she said. "I looked at him and had a terrifying realization— he was dead. I started crying and asked, 'How is this happening, Grandpa? You are dead.' He looked over at me and held my hand and said, 'I'm okay, Amy. It's okay. I'm okay.' I awoke in tears, but I also woke up knowing that somehow, that was him," she said. "And what's so strange is that I encounter people all the time who swear they have spoken to a deceased loved one, in a dream or otherwise, and so many of them say the same thing: 'I'm okay.'"

If you are going to receive any message in a dream from a loved one who has passed, "I'm okay" seems to be one that we need the most. Amy felt guilt over how things were left with her grandfather, and this dream provided some closure. Maybe that's the reason why these dreams occur? Spirits who love us know what we need, so they come back to us in what may be the simplest way they can, in order to ease our fears, guilt, or regrets about the situation or how it was left in the end.

I don't know what it takes for a ghost to communicate with us in a dream or to interact with us in the real world. I suspect, if the biblical sleep and afterlife theory is more true than not, it would be efficient, and require less energy, to get your loved one's attention in a dream world rather than trying to stand at the foot of their bed in the middle of the night and deliver a message, like something out of a Charles Dickens novel.

Visitation Dreams as Support for the Living

My childhood friend Melissa is one of the strongest people I know. We have been friends since we were six years old, and grew up performing together, snatching all the theater, band, and choir trophies we could along the way.

Melissa has had to cope with two great losses in her life. Her father passed away when she was twenty-three, and she lost the love of her life, her husband Heath, to a heart condition just a few years later. Ben and I met Heath during those few years they had together and I will never forget his kindness and how welcoming he was. I was introducing Ben to where I grew up in Alabama during this trip, and I was uncertain how people would react to our relationship. Heath was a breath of fresh air, a light that shone so much kindness into the darkness of my fear. Beyond that, seeing the two of them together, and witnessing the many things they were doing as a couple for the community, was something to behold.

After Heath passed away, I remember sitting across from Melissa at a dinner I will never forget. She said, "I'm a widow before thirty. How is that even imaginable?" Those words and the weight of what she was dealing with were immeasurable.

After his passing, Melissa had many dreams about Heath—and she wasn't the only one. Two of their close friends were experiencing the same thing at the same time, and all the dreams had a common theme. "These dreams with Heath were always centered around sharing a meal at a table," she said. "Always. Something significant to Heath, and his walk with God, was the idea of communion and how there's always room at the table. He loved sharing meals with people. Sharing a meal was just always an important part. That was that relational piece that he felt was so important and so missing. It was a way for him to commune with God, too. So, it's just interesting that in my dreams and our friends' dreams, we were always, at some point, at a table together. We met at a table, you know?"

Melissa's dream didn't consist of all of their friends together, at a table, in the same dream. She would be alone, privately, with Heath each time. Every friend had that singular moment, in a dream with Heath, sitting at a table. Growing up in the South and going to church, food and fellowship were always at the forefront of our community activities. Every Sunday, after church, there would be a feast in the community room that could feed an entire village. It was a way to connect with each other and check in on our friends. For our elderly congregation, it might have been their only source of companionship for the week, and a way to supplement their basic needs with two or three takeaway containers. In our community, food brought us together, and breaking bread with one another was not just a symbol of faith; it was a connection to God and family.

"What was interesting, when I looked at Heath, it was him in this really beautiful, restored form," Melissa said. "He was strong. He wasn't pale and weak. When he was sick, he was in pain a lot and slowly losing weight and very pale. But, in every dream, he just looked so healthy and so alive. I remember a couple of times he was walking towards me, coming down a long hallway, and it was a really good feeling. I remember one night, he embraced me and it was an intimate dream and I just remember feeling so many emotions and thinking, *I have missed you.*"

As she spoke to me, I could see the moment playing out for her, in her eyes, her face, the way she touched her arm and put her hands gently together. She was reliving a moment so pure that it was etched into every fiber of her being. "I could feel his skin," she described. "I can still tell you what his skin feels like today. Like, the feel of his freckles. I could feel that in the dream. I could feel him holding me. I could feel the familiarity, the smell of him. It was just so visceral. It's the closest thing I could get to actually seeing him again."

One of the more interesting aspects of visitation dreams is touch, which is a common theme in many of these dreams. Spirits touching, hugging, or interacting physically could be a way to form a deeper connection in the moment. Maybe it's because a familiar touch is undeniable. Other times, those who are having the dream experience, reach out to touch the hand of the person and it goes away, or they go to hug them and the person who has passed pulls away—as if to make a statement that they are no longer available to communicate physically that way anymore.

She paused for a moment as she returned from the memory. In more than thirty years of friendship, I had never seen Melissa like that before. I was in awe of her understanding and resolve in knowing that Heath was okay. When I looked at her, there was no doubt in my mind that what she experienced was true, real, and life affirming. "I had those dreams, especially early on, pretty regularly," she said. "Then it slowly dissipated and didn't happen anymore after that."

Then he was gone, off to continue the journey, or, as he would have wanted most, to take his place in the kingdom of God. Melissa had these dreams not once, not twice, but nearly a dozen times. Each time, they helped her heal some of the trauma she was carrying with her.

I asked her if she got any practical information from Heath. Selfishly, as a paranormal researcher, I wanted to know if he imparted any knowledge that we could all carry with us. "Just comfort," she said, "like, 'I love you. I'm okay. I do miss you. I wish I could be there, but also things are really good here and I'm still with you.'"

Most visitation dreams seem to be geared toward the feelings and emotional journey of those who are still living. But, are these life-altering dreams solely for the purpose of the living, or do some spirits use this opportunity to fulfill needs of their own? Is there knowledge to be gained from these dreams that give us tangible information about what happens after we die?

Visitation Dreams as Closure for the Dead

My friend Yvette had a dream visitation that hit her at the core of her soul. Yvette and I have been friends since my first year of college. When she was twenty-three, she was in a successful band, living the dream, and making a name for herself in New York City. Her boyfriend at the time was also in the band, along with their mutual friend Patrick. (I have changed his name for privacy.) Patrick was an extremely talented musician. He attended one of the most prestigious music schools in New York City, receiving one of only two full scholarships.

A few years into their friendship, on April Fool's Day, Yvette and her boyfriend started receiving messages and texts that Patrick had passed away. "It was just all of a sudden and it was so shocking," she said. His roommate had come home to the apartment and found him unresponsive on the couch. The autopsy revealed that he had taken a mixture of uppers and downers—though Patrick had never shown any signs that he was using any sort of drugs.

Everyone who knew him thought it was very strange. He had just broken up with his girlfriend and was going through something emotional, but this was extremely out of the ordinary. While he did drink alcohol and would party like anyone else his age, the chemicals they found in his system were the equivalent of substances like heroin or cocaine. There was suspicion, at least in their circle of friends, surrounding this death.

"Right after he passed away, we went to his funeral and his family was all there and they didn't want anybody to know about the drugs," she said. "They wanted everyone to think he just died of natural causes. And I remember it began snowing the second they started putting his body in the ground. This was in April, so it was maybe a little bit late for snow? I remember that feeling of thinking, *Wow, this is really weird that it's snowing right now.*"

Sometimes those strange, out of place moments, are the ones you remember most. When an experience like that is coupled with a dream visitation, you can't help but take notice of it. "Right around that time was the first visit that I got from him when I was sleeping," Yvette said. "Part of me knew that it was real and not a dream. When I first saw him, because it felt so real, I kept saying to him, 'You're not supposed to be here, you're not supposed to be here.'"

She was afraid. To her, it was like seeing a ghost for the first time, and not just any ghost, but a full-body apparition of someone she loved, standing in front of her. She wanted to run away screaming. "He would say, 'I really need to talk to you,'" Yvette recalled. "And I would be really, really terrified and I would just say, 'No, no, no, no, no, no.' I would wake up drenched in sweat, just like super anxious, thinking, *What was that?*"

I would classify this as a paranormal experience. As someone who had never dealt with anything like that before, Yvette tried to rationalize it, telling herself it was just a dream and trying to put the whole experience behind her. However, Patrick was persistent.

"Like a day later he came back to me in a dream," she explained. "The same thing happened. I'd start saying to him, 'You're not supposed to be here.' And he would say, 'Yvette, you have an awareness where you can speak to people when we're in this certain realm, and I need your help.'"

I think that some of us are open and more prone to paranormal activity, even if we aren't aware of it and aren't trying to cultivate it in our lives. Chip Coffey says we are all a little bit psychic, we just need to access that part of our brain. I think because we are all made up of the same energy, we all are capable of being affected by paranormal experiences in different ways.

Sometimes you won't recognize the experience because maybe it seems insignificant. In Yvette's case, it was a massive, unavoidable situation. "I was like, 'Okay, what can I do?' He said, 'It's just me. You should never have to be afraid of me,'" she said. "He had calmed me down at this point and he said, 'I have some messages that I need to get out to friends and family.' He said, 'I know you're really skeptical about whether this is a dream or whether this is real. So, I want to leave you with some information so that when you wake up you can clarify that this isn't just a dream.'"

Patrick told Yvette to go to her partner at the time and ask him about a show they played together in Vermont. He told her to ask him if he remembered a song they played together during this set, along with a few other details about that specific night, that exact show, in that precise location. Her partner had been skeptical of the first dream, attributing it to the fact that Patrick's death was so recent and that his friends were all thinking of him and dreaming about him. She laid out all of the detailed information as instructed, waiting for a reaction that would determine if what was happening in her dreams was indeed real.

"My partner went completely white," she said. "He was just like, 'What the fuck? That's crazy.' It's not something that I could have known. I wasn't there and I'd never heard the story. That's when I knew that this was a thing." It was all the confirmation Yvette needed in order to accept that what she was dealing with was not a figment of her imagination.

But Patrick wasn't done. "He came back to me again for a third time and he said, 'Did you get your confirmation?' And I said, 'Yeah, I got the confirmation.' Then he said, 'I have some really important things I need to tell you. It's really important for my family to know that I didn't intend to overdose. I didn't take a lot of it. I just had a really bad reaction to it.'"

Yvette explained to me that Patrick had a surgery a few years prior to fix a medical issue with his esophagus, which had to do with sections of it being narrower than should be. "I think I connected the fact that his esophagus, in combination with the bad reaction, was the reason why he died," she continued. "What he explained to me was he had felt sick, but then couldn't properly throw up when he was in that state where he was not fully conscious. He said, 'I don't want my friends and my family to think that I killed myself or that I was taking drugs on a regular basis. I was just really, really depressed about my breakup.'"

At this point Yvette paused briefly as if she was reliving the moment once again. You can't *not* be fundamentally changed when a spiritual experience occurs that is so undeniably real. Like my first experience in Gettysburg, Yvette, in her mind, was given undeniable proof that ghosts or something like ghosts were real. Patrick had one last confirmation for Yvette before this third dream was over. "He then said, 'I want you to tell everybody that I'm here and I was the snow at my funeral.'" Yvette said that this sent chills down her spine. She had thought it was weird that it was snowing so late into April, and she'd been right.

Yvette's hardest challenge with the experience was what to do with the information she had been given. Patrick was very clear that he wanted his family and friends to all know the truth surrounding his death. She got all that information, but from a visitation dream—not everyone would be receptive to that. Imagine how hard that would be. It's challenging enough when I have to talk about ghosts and my experiences with strangers, but to have to relay messages from a spirit to a family that didn't ask for your help, and tell them it came in a dream, but it's the truth as told by Patrick.... That's another level.

The information wasn't bad—in my eyes it would be helpful—but the hard part was how that information would be received. It could reopen healing wounds, or damage Yvette's relationships with those people. Yvette emailed Patrick's sister and told her the entire story. "I think she was semi-receptive to it, but not as receptive as I would've liked her to be," she said. "She was just like, 'Oh, okay, well thanks, thank you.' Maybe she just didn't believe it to be true or believe it was possible or something. So, I left it like that with her."

It's a personal decision what any of us would have done in that situation. I, for one, would feel like I had to follow through with Patrick's request. Even though I would be scared of how his family would react, I would need to finish the task. Others may think there would be no way that they could tell the family that kind of information, even if they felt the experience was real. I think the big push for Yvette to follow through was the reoccurrence of the dream visitation. One dream, and she might have explained it away. Two dreams, and it's a toss-up if you believe it or not. Three dreams is hard to deny. You can't just sit on that. What if the dreams never stopped or Patrick never rested in peace?

Patrick said he chose Yvette because she was able to receive his message. If he had gone to anyone else, the outcome might have been very different. Patrick might still be haunting someone to this day. Closure in many cases is very important to the dead, but what about Yvette? Did what she accomplished make a difference?

"I want to say it was two months before I saw Patrick again," she said. "He came back the last time and he looked different this time. He looked more peaceful. It's almost like he was sharing parts of himself in whatever his next life was, or the next realm was, while also sharing parts of himself with his old life here. So much time had gone by, he had become more divinely suited to the next realm rather than to this one. So, he started to feel less like a person and more like a spirit."

Yvette described this as both a feeling she was getting from him and the experience and as a visual transformation. "When I would first see him, he looked like a regular person in front of me right now," she explained. "But the last time I saw him, he was lighter and also more transparent." The way she described it, what once was flesh and blood, in look and feeling, was becoming ethereal and connected to the hereafter.

"The last time I saw him, I just remember thinking, *You're still around? How does this work?*" she said. "I had so many questions for him about the afterlife, but he didn't really want to give me too much information. It's almost like we're not supposed to know, or he wanted to protect me from knowing too much." Incredibly fascinating to me, but also really frustrating. If only spirits would just come out and tell us everything we need to know and be done with it. Yvette had a ton of reasons to believe him up to this point, so why not give her the ultimate security of the truth behind the afterlife? She felt that she wasn't supposed to know because as living humans, we wouldn't even be able to grasp what it's like.

This lines up with my own experience of trying to communicate with spirits about the afterlife. Amy and I have investigated places where we have asked ghosts if they are in heaven or someplace like it, and we rarely get a response. I think of it as trying to verbally explain a sunset to someone, or to put into words an

160

incredibly moving experience. Maybe those spirits are truly at a loss for words, so when a spirit is asked to explain the unexplainable, they can't. Their experience might be that of a sunset, a feeling, a moment, and there are no words for it, no written vocabulary for us to comprehend.

Or it could be that Patrick's afterlife, where he is now and how he got there, is completely and very specifically his own and no one else's. Just like each visitation dream is unique and singular, maybe each death and afterlife experience is singular as well. However, Patrick did drop a few nuggets of knowledge. "He said that the afterlife was less straightforward and more random," Yvette said. "The way I understood it was that some people, when they pass, just go straight to the next thing. For him, he felt like he had things that he wanted to say and do here to try and complete before that happened. He affirmed the fact that energy doesn't die, it transfers, and that we're all on these journeys. What that felt like to me, in the moment, was his spirit was going somewhere else where you wouldn't see or feel him the same way anymore. It felt like spirits are always around, but in a different shape."

If anyone ever needed a bit more information on what it might be like when we die, directly from the source, this would be a good time to take notes. Of course, we take everything with a grain of salt, and this is one person's visitation experience, but there are correlations between what Patrick was telling her and what I see when spirits have unfinished business. His death was tragic, sudden, and more than likely accidental. He had just cause to be here until he could complete a mission that would not only help and comfort his friends and family, but would provide closure for himself. He got lucky that Yvette was so open to the experience. I've seen many spirits who have passed and are ignored until paranormal investigators come along.

With the huge number of people who die every day and the limited amount of actual paranormal investigators in the world, I think those who are receptive to spirit communication and know how to receive their messages are like a needle in a haystack for ghosts. To me, the most interesting thing Patrick said was the part about the transfer of energy, that energy doesn't die, it just goes somewhere else. That's a scientific maxim, and to hear it from someone who's transitioning to the next phase of being is impactful.

Patrick's final message to Yvette was this: "My time in the in-between is done. I'm getting ready to transition and I'm happy and I'm okay. I want you to know that there is life beyond this, and you're not going to see me again, like this, anymore." What I want to consider with his entire final goodbye—the collective energy, the unfinished business, the clear message that life does exist beyond this one—is how Patrick's story connects with what I am doing right now. I'm writing and you're reading his story in his words. Maybe he even knew one day his story would be used in a bigger way so that it would affect more people than his one dear friend.

Yvette first told me about all of this very shortly after it happened, long before I was seriously pursuing the paranormal field. Back then, it was still a hobby for me and I had no idea what my own future would hold in this world. But maybe Patrick did? It could have been a tiny seed planted for the bigger picture and more impactful purpose. If everything is energy and we are all connected, possibly that's true. Spirits worry about their legacy being unrecognized, or being forgotten. Well, Patrick, if your legacy and bigger purpose in the afterlife is getting this message to the world, I am humbled that Yvette told me about you all those years ago and has now allowed me to share it with the world. Who knows? Maybe this is the rest of Patrick's grand finale.

What if visitation dreams are rare because a lot of us don't talk about them to other people, or only share them with our closest confidantes? These dreams are intimate, real, and very personal. Death and grief can be hard to discuss, especially when your process of grieving doesn't line up to how, or how quickly, other people expect you to work through your loss.

Visitation Dreams that Help with Healing

Visitations like these are part of that grieving process. My hope is that people start to normalize talking about these moments with each other, because we may find that there are more commonalities between all of them than we've realized. Melissa and her friends had the common thread of sitting at a table with Heath. After her father passed away, she had a dream that her father called her on the phone to say that he loved her and that everything was all right. Melissa's brother had the exact same dream on the same night. The dreams mirrored each other and they would have never known that each of them had that same visitation if Melissa hadn't casually brought it up in conversation.

When I was preparing for this book, I spoke with two of my aunts on a trip to Vermont. I talked about the subject matter of the book, but specifically told them about the visitation dream that I had about my grandmother, their mother. My aunt Wanda then spoke of a visitation that happened shortly after Grannie passed, where she came to Wanda in the dream and said, "I'm not dead. The doctors got it all wrong." While Wanda was telling her story, my aunt Rita chimed in and said, "Oh my! I had the same dream, but I have never told anyone, ever."

In their dreams, Grannie said the same thing to each of them and they both tried to get her to go to the doctor to prevent her from getting worse. Wanda's dream ended in the process of the checkup, and Rita's dream concluded with Grannie passing once more. They both said that the dream was real and vivid, as if it was actually happening. My aunts were able to bond and heal over a similar shared experience, even though it was eight years after their mother's death. It might have helped them to process a little part of their grief a bit sooner if they had spoken about the dreams when they happened. I think sharing our visitation dreams is a way of coping with loss, not just on a personal level, but also collectively through support and healing with others who have lost that person, too.

By now you are probably wondering if I'm going to talk about my own visitation dream. I thought about not including it in this book; it is very special to me and I have rarely talked about it publicly. Also, I believe that if you speak a dream out loud, you won't have that dream again. I've had reoccurring nightmares before and as soon as I tell someone about them, they seem to not happen again. I have reservations that I may not have the dream again. But in this instance, and for the sake of collective healing, I'm going to practice what I preach.

Everything around me was a grayish blue haze, almost like the ocean, but without any deep sea pressure. I was standing somewhere, on *something*, but there were no walls or doors around me, no floor beneath me, nothing whatsoever in my view. I found myself in a vastness that went far past my field of vision, but somehow, I knew that my surroundings had no ending. I wasn't afraid: I knew I could be there, and I felt welcomed. The only thing I can compare it to is like being on a massive movie soundstage, where the lights are just bright enough that you can't really see anything past them, but you know the space extends far beyond.

I was only there for a brief moment before I saw her. As I adjusted to new shapes and soft lights forming in front of me, I began to make out details of who she was. She was wearing a pastel nightgown that seemed familiar, with cozy slippers to match, and she manifested from nowhere to make her way toward me. As the ambient light graced her face, I knew instantly who she was: my grannie, who had passed away only a few months earlier.

She seemed to radiate peace and knowledge, and projected a forthright confidence. In the instant I recognized her, I knew she was all right. Instead of looking sickly as she did at the end of her life, she was healthy and happy. Her appearance was just as I remembered most of my life. It was also immediately clear to me that she knew what was happening was a real moment, and that it was being allowed to happen through divine permission. It was special, as if she was granted this time so that I could have this experience.

Grannie slowly walked toward me, and as she got closer, I felt myself gently falling backwards. I came to rest on my back, looking up into the abyss. Standing over me, she reached out her hands and I took hold of them. We gripped each other's hands. Then I put both feet against her and she leaned forward, lifting into the air. As a kid, my brother and friends and I would call this "flying." In our imagination, we were soaring above the clouds to the highest mountain tops. In recreating this childhood game, my grannie was flying directly above me.

Then, I spoke six words to her: "What do you do all day?"

She looked at me a little puzzled. "What?" she asked softly, as if trying to understand words again.

I repeated myself. "What do you do all day?"

She paused and said softly, "I make deliveries."

I replied in the same way as she did the first time. "What?"

Slowly and with intention, as to separate each word a little bit more, she said, "I...make...deliveries."

Looking at her shining face, I somehow knew exactly what she meant. Deliveries, I thought, yes. It was in this moment of my understanding, she got a slightly puzzled look on her face, as if something had changed, or maybe she felt different, or perhaps she knew something was coming. She began to pull away as if there was a string coming out of her back.

I was afraid at first, and a little disturbed, maybe frightened, by the sudden shift of energy. It wasn't fast, though—it was gentle, and she didn't seem scared. She knew what was happening. We held on to each other's hands so tightly. I could feel the coarseness of the skin of her hands, which had experienced so much life and had held so many people.

I suddenly became aware that this was most likely the last time I would see her, at least in this life. I could tell in her eyes that she knew it too. I didn't want to let go, but I knew I didn't have the power or strength to keep her with me. The cord that was attached to her kept pulling, her body contorting from the tug, but the two of us were just holding on so tight. In a moment, a blink, at the same instant I knew we could hold on no longer, I awoke from my sleep. It was done and she was gone.

I felt a flood of different emotions, but I understood the entire experience. It needed to happen, and, in a way, I felt lucky to have it. "Deliveries," I said out loud. What was she delivering? Babies? Packages? Maybe, deliverance? She was a religious woman. Perhaps, she was given her wings and became an angel for the purpose of delivering messages. After all, the word angel comes from the ancient Greek *angelos*, meaning messenger.

Maybe her purpose was to set me free, to release me from any unfinished business or guilt I was carrying. I wasn't there with her when she passed due to unavoidable circumstances. I did record a message for her to be played by her bedside, and I said everything I needed to say. But in the back of my mind, I always thought I should have been there to say goodbye, to hold her hand one last time.

Whatever this encounter was, I never had that experience again. That was truly the last time my grannie visited me to give me information and the last time we had such a strong afterlife connection. I've seen her since in a few dreams, but I never have any control over what's happening. Nowadays if I see her in a dream, it's more like a memory, a vehicle in which I am a passenger rather than the driver. This event changed me. It eased my fears about her state of being and it cracked through the armor of grief that was weighing me down at the time. Sometimes when you least expect it, miracles happen. Tiny miracles that push you through and keep you going. Giving everyone the chance to fly.

CHAPTER 11

Dealing with Grief in Life and the Afterlife

The grief that comes with the passing of a loved one is something I don't think ever goes away completely. But if we don't work to come to terms with it, grief can consume us.

In the midst of all that pain and loss, there are lessons to be learned from grieving. In processing the feelings that come from loss, we often find a pathway to a better understanding and acceptance of life's challenges in general. We can forge stronger bonds with the people in our lives or appreciate small things in a deeper way. We can learn more about ourselves and the world around us. For a few, their process of healing was creation: some of the paranormal equipment we use in our investigations was created by people whose personal grief inspired them to invent tools to help communicate with those they had lost.

Dealing with grief can be isolating and lonely, and like most burdens, it's more easily carried when it's shared. Sometimes we need a friend or partner to shine a light into the emptiness, flashing a glimmer of warmth into our soul so that we know there is a pathway out.

Shortly before writing this book, Ben and I faced a crushing loss. As any pet owner will tell you, the death of a beloved pet can be just as devastating as the loss of a fellow human. They live in our homes with us, sharing our every moment, giving unconditional love and affection. These beautiful animals are interconnected with our own existence. So, when they leave us, it feels like there is a void that's impossible to fill. Maria, our oldest, was one year old when I met Ben. Cheeto, our youngest, was adopted a couple years after. They are truly part of the family, and we love them like they are our children.

Our chihuahua Maria passed on October 30, 2022, at seventeen. By all standards, she lived a long and happy life: our baby girl was a doted-on chichi and a well-traveled fashionista who made friends wherever she went. She looked like a tiny baby deer, who only weighed three pounds but who would run with the big dogs. Maria had been in failing health for two years, and we knew eventually she would let us know it was her time to go, but it didn't make that loss any easier.

That weekend, Ben and I went to Salem, Massachusetts—the town calls itself Witch City, after the Salem Witch Trials of 1692—to stay at the haunted Hawthorne Hotel for our annual Halloween trip. We go to Salem many times throughout the year, and this place feels like a second home. Maria was our little witch, especially in Salem. Over the years we noticed she had a spark when we were in Witch City, and later in life, more pep in her step. It was as if she were casting spells on everyone, practicing doggie magick when we weren't looking.

As this weekend progressed, we noticed she was more lethargic and eating less. We knew it was getting close to her time; our vet had told us at our last visit that her medicine was no longer working and there was nothing else we could do. But we wanted to love and support her as much as we could on this journey, and to let her go naturally and peacefully, without the aid of an injection.

We held her close and laid with her. "The need to distract myself is massive," I wrote at the time, wanting to remember this grief. "Thinking of things to do in a spiritual way while her death is happening seems to be one of them. What ritual can we do? What incense can we light or prayer and incantation can we say? The urge to leave the hotel to have a moment away from the grief is strong as well, but that's hard to do as we want to be with her constantly to comfort. However, if Maria is holding on for us then we need to give her space to transition if she wants. I spoke with her and let her know it's okay to go, that it's all right. Tears flowed freely and fast."

Ben and I left for about an hour that evening to get something to eat. We hoped that by giving her privacy, she would feel free to let go—but she was still holding on when we got back. We had no choice but to go to an emergency vet. We wrapped her up in one of her favorite cozy blankets, put a small piece of rose quartz into the zip pocket of her warm sweater, and prepared to say good bye.

It was my first time ever having to make this choice for a pet, but even if you've gone through it before, I don't think anyone is ever truly ready to face what comes next. We held her, we loved on her, we cried so hard. I found myself apologizing to her and saying, "We love you baby girl," over and over. At 10:45 p.m., Maria was gone. In the moments after her last heartbeat, my chest hurt and it was hard to breathe, like my heart wasn't just broken, it was gone.

I was still holding Maria, wrapped in her blanket, when Ben said to me, "I see her. I can see her jumping up and down next to you, like she used to do."

Later, Ben described more of what he saw at the vet's office. "She was there with us as a young dog, acting the way she used to greet you coming home from long cases and trips," he explained. "Out of nowhere, she came running into the room and was jumping on her back feet towards you, but you were still holding her body in the blanket. She hadn't been able to move around like that for years.

"It felt like I was seeing her ghost," Ben said. "It also was exactly what I needed in that moment. I saw and felt something that let me know that she was okay." This could have been a crisis apparition. He saw a vision of Maria, at the time of her passing, saying goodbye one last time. While these experiences are normally documented as distant encounters, with the loved one passing from far away yet appearing right in front of you, the paranormal is unpredictable. He felt her presence, and he knew she was sending us a message. She was there for him to witness in a powerful way. I didn't see her, but I knew Ben was right. She was full of life again, ready to run on the beach with Petie and Lucky, two of her canine friends who had preceded her. She was free from pain and sickness.

I don't think it was a coincidence that our girl picked Salem as the place, and Halloween of all the times, to transition into the next life. Maybe she knew something we didn't. The veil is thinner at that time and place. The spirits are alive. And Maria wasn't our little witch anymore. She was our little angel.

The next day was Halloween, and we did the best we could to celebrate Maria's life and our favorite holiday. It happened to be the most beautiful day, and we took comfort that it was her spirit making it so. We made our phone calls and spent the day reminiscing, having a few martinis, people watching—and most importantly, showering all our love on Cheeto, who was grieving in his own way.

We were still filming season seven of *Kindred Spirits*, and I was on camera less than two days after for an episode in Gettysburg. The days were filled with work, but the nights were harder as we sat with our thoughts. Pets only hurt us once, when they die, and they don't even mean to do it. Ben and I supported one another, and our friends were incredibly generous with their time and talks. Grief can be crippling and truly has a mind of its own, but we found comfort in knowing that the time we had with her outweighed not having her in our lives at all. We slowly shifted our mindset to celebrating the moments of joy and happiness we shared with her, rather than focusing on the trauma of the ending. There will never be another soul like her, ever, and I feel so humbled and fortunate that her little spirit found her way to us. Maria's passing left a void in our lives.

I've also experienced real and deep grief from the loss of friends and loved ones. The passing of both my grandmothers left holes in my heart and in my family. And I've lost dear friends, whose deaths, expected or not, felled me. In those times, I was left grasping for understanding.

One of those friends gone too soon is Tim McCarthy, who was among the first people I met when I moved to Provincetown. He was an activist and documentarian, and one of the most exciting and genuinely kind people I have ever met. I rented a room in his home the summer of 2006, when I met Ben. Now Ben and I are renting the house for the winter while I finish this book. It's a full circle moment for our relationship. What better way to write a book on grief, loss, and the paranormal, than being surrounded by the energy and memory of someone who meant so much to me?

You might assume that I would take personal loss a little easier than most. After all, I'm surrounded by death every day, and my entire career focuses on the afterlife. While I definitely do find comfort in what I know about ghosts and what we experience in our investigations, I'm only human. I feel things very deeply and I am still susceptible to the realities of a loved one's passing and the weight of the grief that comes with that loss.

Those feelings are rooted in the knowledge that I will never see them again in their physical bodies—never feel the warmth of their touch, hear their laugh, go on an adventure with them, or hear their voice on the other end of the phone. I have an unusual appreciation for how easy it is to communicate with each other in this life, something that's easy for people to take for granted, because of how challenging it is to communicate with the non-living.

In investigations, we aren't promised anything from the other side. We can't demand results. We can only do our best to try and make a connection with those who have passed. Maybe that is why I don't try to reach out to people I am close to after they are gone. Part of it is definitely, as I mentioned before, that I'm worried that they may need or want something that I can't provide.

Another part of it is that when they were alive, I could just pick up the phone. Now, it's a million times less likely I'll be able to reach them. I don't reach out because part of me is afraid they won't respond. There's a real likelihood that I could try and try, but never find the right frequency. That would be like losing them all over again, another loss piled on the original one. And on top of that, I would feel like I have failed at the thing I do best. That's why I think I would prefer they come to me.

Kathy Kelly shared a story with me that she hasn't told many people, about a connection she had after she lost someone close to her. "My dearest friend in the world, someone I met at ten years old and knew for thirty-three years, died," she explained. "To say I was devastated would be an absurd understatement. It was world-shattering for me at the time. And even though I had been a paranormal student for thirty years at that point, I still was at a loss to understand and accept the depth of my grief. Nothing prepared me for it. It wasn't my first loss, but it was a fresh one.

"Her death was not unexpected, but still was shocking," Kathy continued. "I was completely bereft." This friend had passed way too young, from an illness that took her life in two short months. After her funeral, Kathy and her wife took the vacation to Mexico that they had been planning before her friend passed. The last time they visited the country, it had been with that friend.

"I remember one night, a mere two weeks after her death, being in our hotel suite and crying," Kathy said. "I was more than sad, I was enraged, too. I could not wrap my head around her death, or at that moment, death at all." She found herself asking why any of this had to happen, why we had to lose people we love so much. "I knew better than to look to the universe for those kinds of answers, but I was so very angry and sad and lost," Kathy continued. "I looked at my wife and I said, 'But where is she? Where is she?' My faith in everything was gone, my understanding of the nuances of experience was shattered, and I just needed an answer.

"My wife sat there looking at me, crying too, shaking her head... and then I just said, 'I don't get it? Where did her life go? Where is her spirit? Where is *she*?'" Kathy said. "Suddenly without preamble or warning, every single light in the suite turned off. Zip. Off. We sat in quiet, surprised silence. I then said, 'Did that just happen? Maybe it's a power outage.' As I said that, one single lamp turned back on."

They were sure something important was happening in that room. "As I write this I realize that I cannot convey the oddness or the impact of that moment, except to say that we were convinced at that moment that we had experienced the spiritual and the paranormal," she added. "I almost never tell this story because I don't want to commercialize it or have it become a 'tale.' It's so personal and so meaningful to me. But Adam asked and he is very meaningful to me, too."

A sign from a loved one in a time of grief can be powerful indeed. My thinking is that if those I have lost don't reach out to me, then they must be at peace. Although the silence may be deafening, it needs to be appreciated for what it is: the serenity of a spirit who was fortunate enough to have left no unfinished business behind. As much as we ache to hear from our departed loved ones again, there isn't a better outcome for them than to be fully at peace in the afterlife. The silence may also be a sign that they sense you don't actually need comfort and confirmation from them, or perhaps that someone else needs it more.

So, remember, if you don't get a sign from a loved one who has passed on, don't be discouraged. It likely means they are in a good place. As you know, our paranormal cases generally involve spirits who want something they can't get for themselves. They are often in a heightened state of agitation, confusion, aggression, or loneliness. No one would want that for a departed loved one. If you're trying to connect and you don't get a response, remember that they are on their next journey, and that if they need to reach you, they know where to find you. You can keep them in your heart and mind, holding their memory close and keeping yourself open and receptive to the idea that a sign may come when you least expect it.

Grief Through a Psychic Lens

Tyler Henry, a world-renowned psychic medium, knows a great deal about how we cope with death and loss. He has spent many years using clairvoyance to connect grieving loved ones with those who have passed on. He creates a direct connection to the afterlife that can provide answers, comfort, and a deeper understanding and acceptance of things. I wanted to know if his connection with those who have passed on gave him any insight into how they felt about the grief of the living.

"I would say that I have learned that grief is a universal process," Tyler said. "Something we can't escape no matter what our spirituality or beliefs might be. I think we grieve the dead more than they grieve us. And that might sound kind of strange, but it seems like when people come through, they feel more connected to their loved ones. They feel more connected to their sense of humanity, while ironically having had to part with a very fundamental part of being human: their body. So that alone is some insight into grief."

I think when we pray, meditate, or simply sit quietly remembering those we have lost, it's actually a very important part of processing grief that brings us a little bit closer to healing each time we do it. I have always believed that that work does some good on both sides of the veil, and that the spirits feel it as well when we think of them or say their name; it brings them back to our side for a moment.

Tyler said that he's learned something from those he's spoken to in the afterlife who have given him really good advice. "I think having an understanding that there's no escaping [death] is a good start to the grief process," he explained. "One of the greatest takeaways I have received from people who've died tragically is their insistence that we are so much more than how we died, and that a human being shouldn't be defined by a single moment in time. So, when we remember them as they were in life, it does us good and it does them good.

"Basically, the more we focus on all the happy moments with that person, the sooner we will heal," Tyler said. "A practical goal to have is getting to a place where we are more inclined to smile than to cry when we think of our departed loved ones. Just because we are smiling doesn't mean that all the pain is gone. And getting there takes time. But it helps to keep that reachable goal in mind."

For those grieving the loss of a loved one who don't have access to experts in communicating with the dead, there are still potential ways of connecting with spirits in the afterlife without outside help. But it requires a lot of persistence and patience. As Tyler Henry observes, it involves a sort of quid pro quo of effort from both sides. "I think this idea of meeting them in the middle is very important," he said. "People expect after someone passes, because they're in such a state of desperation, to get hit over the head with a sign. For many, that is seldom the case. But we can put in the effort to meet spirits in the middle—through processes of self-awareness, journaling, meditation, and mindfulness. All these things are tools in our toolkit to position ourselves to make that spiritual connection we so desperately want to make. But it is a process. And I think fundamentally we have to grieve before anything."

So, don't be afraid to grieve or open yourself up spiritually through self-awareness, and don't focus too hard on a sign that they are with you. It may happen if you are prepared and willing to receive the experience, and if your loved one has something they want to communicate. Mindset and intention are crucial. I tell people this all the time when I am on group paranormal investigations. I usually ask everyone to take three deep breaths all together, so that we can collectively focus on what we are about to do, and clear our minds of day-to-day thoughts. "Be open and willing to have an experience and don't expect it," I tell them. "You will know it when it happens."

If you have had a profound paranormal experience with a deceased loved one, either by yourself, through an investigation, or by having a reading with a psychic medium, it could easily be tempting to continue to try and reach out to have another interaction and reconnect. It may seem like a long-term solution to easing your grief, but it's important to not become dependent on it. And remember, sometimes when a deceased loved one is still around and causing activity, they might be doing it to show you they are still with you, but more than likely they are interacting because they need something for themselves.

It will, of course, bring you comfort to hear from them and I think they know that. However, when the message is received and they are content, they may move on by themselves. I like to encourage people to try and use that first encounter as a stepping stone to continue to process their grief. It's a tool that can be used to help on your journey of recovery from grief, not to stay in the same place.

Another downside to continuing to reach out to the person you lost is that a failure to reestablish contact could trigger your sadness and loss all over again. You may start to wonder if you did something wrong. For me, the what ifs could be anxiety inducing.

Hopefully, at some point you will experience the sensation of knowing that a departed loved one is okay by recognizing little signs that come up from time to time. These signs are special, but they're special because they're rare. Rather than trying to seek them out, I think it's better to let the experience come to you and enjoy it for what it is, however brief. Let them happen where they may, but don't fight to have them every day. Having paranormal encounters in general is like a drug, you just want more and more—believe me, I know. And when these experiences are connected to a person you have lost and are grieving over, it can be an overwhelmingly addictive combination.

Tyler added a bit of advice to aid in the continuation of your grief journey. "I often do readings for people who will have a very evidentiary experience," he said. "Oftentimes it's the skeptics who are transformed in those moments, and then really don't know how to process that initial experience, and want to come back next week and the week after and the week after. There's something to be said about being able to show someone that there is a bond there that exists even after the paranormal investigators and the mediums leave. But that bond is to be cultivated through our actions and honoring them, not necessarily by holding on to that human part that has since passed. It may seem like a shortcut to getting past our grief when we can turn on a piece of paranormal equipment or contact a medium. But the reality is, it's not. While those experiences can affirm the inner connection, they will never replace it."

Spirits in a Heightened State

Through our years of investigation, Amy and I have connected with lost loved ones and brought families together again with closure and communication—but we've generally done that in times of distress, both among the living and the dead. The spirits we tend to connect with fit that category of "heightened state." Often, the activity that's happening in the home seems aggressive and unnerving. There are moments the homeowners feel like they are being attacked by an unimaginable force, or the energy of the space feels oppressive and unwelcoming. The living have reached a boiling point, and some are experiencing sheer terror.

When a ghost has been aggressive or threatening, and then it turns out that the spirit is a deceased loved one, the homeowner is often shocked at first. I mean, why would your favorite grandmother aggressively haunt you? It's most likely because the family kept ignoring or tried to banish the spirits or dismiss the activity.

This, in turn, forced their loved one to work even harder to get their attention. If they try too hard it may come off as aggressive or negative—and thinking back to my haunted honey experiment, when I felt such immense pressure and difficulty trying to connect to the living world, I can only assume the spirits feel frustrated and powerless as well. It could also be very easy for a spirit to unintentionally push a little bit too hard trying to connect from the other side and have it feel threatening on our side. We can't begin to understand how they are able to do what they do to interact with the living, but it seems logical to me that sometimes they make mistakes. After all, ghosts are people too.

If someone asks me what case truly epitomizes our mission on *Kindred Spirits*, I always say the same thing: season one, episode eight, called "The Basement." In that episode, Linda and her adult daughter Sandy had lived through an awful trauma. They were on a family trip to Norway when a tragedy occurred. Linda's younger brother Eric, who lived in her basement, had stayed behind to watch the house. Eric was developmentally disabled and absolutely adored by his big sister, and he prided himself in watching over the house while everyone was away.

One night while they were gone, one of Linda's other brothers, who was suffering from addiction, came into the house looking for money. Eric tried to stop him, and things went horribly wrong. His own brother brutally murdered Eric in the basement of the house, the same place that Linda still lives to this day.

When she found out what happened, she was halfway around the world. "I remember that day like it was yesterday," Linda told me recently. "The horror of it all, the brutality of it all. The day that we found out, it was at first pure disbelief. I thought I wasn't hearing right. It was kind of like a horror show. I could never believe....

I knew my brother was really bad, but as far as taking Eric's life.... The tears, the screams. I remember screaming and crying."

Even years after the murder, Linda still can't fully put into words how horrible and traumatic it all was, and still is. "I didn't realize that I was screaming and crying," she said. "The emotions were so strong and horrifying, and I felt like I should have been there. I should have been there to protect him. I should have been there."

"I swear I have PTSD from it, I'll be honest with you," Sandy added. "I don't think I still process it correctly. I don't think any of us do."

Speaking with Linda and Sandy, I could tell that the trauma of this event still felt very near. It's hard enough to process grief when someone passes away naturally, but to have an innocent life taken so suddenly and in such an unfair, unnecessary way—their grief seems compounded by a thousand. Once they returned to the states, Linda lived with Sandy and her family for a little over a month. She couldn't bear to set foot in the house she had lived in for decades out of fear and the weight of this tragedy. "It had to be months before I was even comfortable to walk in this house," she said.

Once she did return home, Linda started experiencing paranormal activity and psychological anomalies she couldn't explain. She began to see a therapist, who tried to help her cope with the guilt of leaving her brother at home and the grief she was experiencing. "I went to a psychiatrist because I would see blood where there was no blood," she said. "My husband would cut himself shaving, and I would freak out."

While the therapy was helping her with her emotions, Linda didn't know who to speak to about the unexplainable things happening in the house that definitely weren't in her head. "In the beginning, I would sleep with all the lights on in the house," she explained. "We would hear noises in the night. We didn't know what these noises were."

For Linda and her family, the paranormal activity that they were facing wasn't just a passing moment of reassurance from a loved one. It seemed to be more intense and widespread. They also didn't know who was trying to reach out. The obvious idea would be Eric, but the things that were occurring didn't seem like him or anyone else they knew who had passed on. Was it him, they wondered, or was it something else that came from the brutal tragedy of his death? Pictures, sconces, and curtains fell off the wall constantly. There were unexplained noises all over the house: knocks, bangs, and footsteps. Doors opened and closed on their own. Linda would see a menacing shadow figure looming over her bed at night and others saw this figure as well. The activity became so severe, especially in the basement, that Linda only went down there once, ever, after they arrived back home. The family even called in a priest to bless the home for fear that something evil might be around. While the prayer gave them a little comfort, it didn't stop the activity. In fact, this bombardment of supernatural phenomena went unexplained for twenty-one years until Amy and I arrived to try and make sense of it all.

The breakthrough in this case, back in 2016, came for Amy and me after I was able to sit down and interview Linda about Eric. I wanted to know if there was anything we could do or say that was specific to Eric, and what he liked or did. Linda told me that he could only count money in one dollar bills and that his favorite thing to play with was Matchbox cars. This detail proved to be very important. When we investigate, we sometimes use a trigger object to make a stronger connection or to get a ghost's attention. This object can be anything, as long as it would be familiar to the person we are trying to reach on the other side.

We headed down to the basement, where Eric was murdered, and where we had been getting some responses but none that were identifiable enough to make us believe it was him. Amy lined up a series of little toy cars, with one a little bit out of line, and a few dollars on the floor; we placed a camera with them so that we could monitor any activity. We sat our recorder down and reached out to Eric.

"I know you might be scared right now," I said, "but there's nobody here that wants to do you harm, okay?" I even mentioned the cars on the floor and the one that Amy purposely left askew. "The yellow car there is a little out of place. It's not in line. Do you want to fix it for us?"

We started hearing footsteps above us, so we left the basement for a brief moment to check it out, leaving the recorder running near the cars and money. When we played back the audio, we heard what sounded like someone saying, "Kapow, vroom." Later when I reviewed our camera footage, one of the dollar bills had been pushed down and completely flattened by an unseen force.

This, for us, was proof Eric was there—but we needed confirmation from Linda. Did the voice on the recorder sound like her brother? We played it for her. She said, "Oh my goodness. That's what Eric would do. He would line his cars up and just like the little kids, he'd make one car go fast and knock into the others."

When we showed Linda and Sandy the dollar bill footage, it became undeniable proof for them that Eric was the one causing the activity. Linda explained that he loved to play pranks, and that knowing it was him made the activity they were experiencing less scary. Looking back on it, she said, those occurrences fit Eric's personality.

During our recent conversation, they both recalled what that moment was like for them. "It was such a relief," Linda said. "I felt that he wasn't gone. He loved playing with his cars and the fact that it was him and that he was happy, it made me happy. I felt comfortable in my home and I had this wave of relief because I always felt that guilt for not being there when he died." She was comforted, she said, "Knowing that he's okay, even though he went through what he went through.

"It's funny," Linda added. "He always treated me like he was my big brother. He always had to take care of me. Knowing that he is still here, I feel like he's still taking care of me. Like, he has to still be the big brother to me even though I'm the oldest sister. That was just Eric." That's a crucial distinction in communicating with loved ones after they pass. It's not that they were reaching out to him or trying to get him to stay—it's that in the afterlife, Eric was choosing to stay behind and be with the family who loved him dearly. When he makes himself known, they make sure to acknowledge that he's there and communicate with him.

Sandy agreed, but expressed her relief for Eric's spirit. "I think part of it for me was, I'm glad to know he's still the Eric we knew," she said. "Still playing and having fun. He was traumatically killed. I was afraid of what he might have been going through if he were still around in spirit. Is he confused? Does he not understand what's going on? Is he scared? Because we don't know what happens after death. I had all these weird worries. So, to hear him took that fear away from me."

The resolution of this case also brought both of them comfort, not only with their grief but also with their own fears about what happens to us after we pass on. For Linda and Sandy, confirming that Eric was still around, playing and being his normal self, gave them hope that the afterlife consists of seeing family again, being able to stay who we are, and retaining parts of our life here on Earth.

Spirit Visitation in Times of Grief

My friend Sarah Coombs is a psychotherapist who helps people process grief and loss from a clinical standpoint, but she had been exploring the paranormal long before she became a licensed therapist. I asked her about the work she does, and whether working through supernatural experiences helps or hinders the healing process.

"When someone comes to me, especially if they have suffered a major loss that just happened, figuring out what their belief systems are around the afterlife is something that I poke in to," Sarah explained. "I find that the people who seem to adjust and process through their grief a little easier seem to be the ones who believe that something goes beyond this life. They feel there is still something that exists of this person beyond this life. It's a comfort to them to know that."

Having faith in an afterlife, that there is something beyond this life and that death isn't finite, is one thing to hold on to when grieving. But when there's more to grief—when there's a layer of the unexplainable attached—things get more complicated. If you're experiencing something paranormal after a loss, and you haven't had anything like that happen before, it could be pretty jarring. If I didn't believe in ghosts, I might think I was going a little bonkers. "Inevitably, if they are going to bring it up, they do within about two or three sessions," Sarah said. "They will say, 'Can I tell you something weird?' I love that every time someone says that, I know they're about to tell me that they saw something or heard something or had some weird thing happen related to the person that they've lost."

Sarah does not market herself as a therapist who helps process grief through the paranormal, but having that extra skill set allows her to take what she knows from a supernatural perspective, meld it with psychological thought and science, and help clients work through the toughest time of their life. Most of these people haven't given ghosts, or paranormal activity, any serious thought. "They will quite often report having seen their loved one, having felt their loved one, viscerally, like no questions, solid as anything," she said. "It's especially interesting to hear about what they experience from people who have no paranormal interest or knowledge. These people, in their grief, will deliberately ask for a sign and they will get it. They are not expecting it. So, it almost lends some credibility that they're having this paranormal experience. They say, 'I saw something out of the corner of my eye, I felt this shift in energy, and then I smelled their cologne.' Like that sort of thing. Then they ask me, 'What is this? Am I going crazy? Is this what happens when I'm grieving?'"

But Sarah sees a lot of clients who experience what could be called visitations while they're grieving. "They're symbolic things, but they defy coincidence for me," she said. "They're just too painful and significant."

A woman came to Sarah shortly after losing her husband, who was young and died unexpectedly. One day, her toddler son got up for no reason, and went to a patch of sunlight, giggling and dancing away. That night, she had a dream about her husband. He said, "I visited you today. I danced with our son in the sunlight."

"When people visit you in your dreams," Sarah said, "they can be symbols of yourself, extensions of self. But there are some dreams where you know for a fact that is your lost loved one and not a symbol or metaphor for anyone or anything else. It just has a different gut feeling."

The same woman later reported sensing her late husband's presence in their house. "She would say, 'I swear he's still hanging around. I swear I see him,'" Sarah explained. "This is someone who's very raw, very vulnerable. I feel like she is primed to potentially be seeing something." One thing Sarah always points out when talking about possible contact from beyond is that severe depression can cause hallucinations, but she didn't think that was happening in this instance.

"If you've just lost your husband, you might actually be majorly depressed and no one would think that was weird," she added. So when does she determine what is just a misfiring of the brain versus an actual paranormal experience?

"Here's the thing," she responded. "I don't believe my job is to figure out which one it is. It doesn't matter. If it's helping them, if they feel like it's bringing comfort, if they feel this is their person saying, 'Hey, I'm still out there. You didn't lose me. I'll always be here,' go with it. It's not doing any harm.

"It was very hard for her," Sarah said of that client. "It was very emotional for her to have these moments. But ultimately, they brought her a lot of joy and comfort."

I've seen investigations in which spirits try to provide some comfort to the living, or finish something they need to do that would both provide closure for the living and allow the spirit to continue its journey. My friend Melissa, who lost her husband Heath and had dream encounters with him, also had an experience while he was still alive, after her father passed away. She was laying on the couch, in grief and pain, and she felt a hand touch her gently on the back of her head. That was exactly what her father would do when she was growing up if she was sick or sad. She knew it was him and felt a small measure of comfort that he was with her in spirit.

"I think whether it's getting evidential information in a ghost hunt or sitting down with a credible medium and receiving a reading, there's something to be said about the confirmation that both of those experiences can provide," Tyler Henry said. "It not only provides the validation that there's a continuation of consciousness beyond physical death, but I think it helps contribute to a conversation that is deeply needed in society. There are so few outlets in the West for us to be able to explore conversations around death and mortality, but more widely, what it means to be alive, what it means to be human. It's a subject that people ignore, but I think it's a testament to why paranormal shows and theories are such a source of interest and intrigue, because people are able to express that deep desire to have those conversations. I think if anything, these gears get turning in people's minds enough in a way to have a transformative effect and approach life differently."

My hope is that there is something beyond and they are there, sometimes reaching out, and are at peace. Then, after it's all said and done, it becomes our turn. If we are one of the lucky ones, we get to live to a very old age and explore a long and happy life, connecting spiritually to the world around us. But is that enough? Have we done enough to be at peace with the last page in our own final chapter? I have hope that we may. Only time will tell.

CHAPTER 12

Living with Death

For most human beings, the idea of death is terrifying, and losing people we love is devastating. But death is a fact of our existence—it's going to happen to everyone. And I think the first step in coping with that harsh reality is to acknowledge that we have no choice but to accept it, live with it, and move forward the best we can.

The next step is to focus on the idea that we are on one journey that takes us to another journey. In a sense, we are paving the way for our afterlife all the time, creating and charging the energy that we will leave behind. I think spirituality helps us build a greater energetic purpose. It focuses our faith in whatever we believe, so that we can get the most out of our true selves. It doesn't have to be faith in an organized religion or even a faith in a higher power. It can be faith in humanity, in our infinite capacity for love and compassion, in connections to each other and the community.

I find solace in trying to connect with those who have already passed and helping where I can. I see it as an act of service to the dead. But I also see it as an act of service to the living. Just speaking from my own experiences, finding evidence of the afterlife and ghosts is truly wondrous. Each encounter shifts my perspective and opens me up to the mysteries of the universe just a little bit more. I hope that, through sharing what I'm learning in this ongoing quest, others can derive comfort from knowing a little bit more about what might be waiting on the other side.

Facing a grim medical prognosis or supporting a loved one through an end-of-life event can be very difficult. I think there's insight to be gained from the stories that follow, individual stories that add to the collective understanding of our shared human existence. We are not alone in our grief, loss, or mourning. Even though at times we may feel the weight of the world is upon us, there have been lifetimes of people who have made this journey before, and we can build upon the pathways they have created.

Tyler Henry had an experience once that echoes this sentiment. While he usually gets requests from grieving family members hoping to reach their loved ones, this call was different. It was about helping a woman come to terms with her own mortality.

"Heather was in her mid-thirties," he explained. "She was happily married with a seven-year-old little boy, and really at a time in her life when everything should have been coming together—but it was falling apart. She had recently been diagnosed with terminal stage four cancer. She knew that even if there were experimental treatments, they weren't likely to work, and she was given only a matter of months to live. So, she contacted me trying to get a reading, to have an understanding of who would be waiting for her when it came time for her to go."

Tyler went to Heather's home and was fully expecting to see someone on their death bed—but she answered the door, looking great, excited for the experience. He said she had even cleaned her entire house. "A number of her loved ones came through in the reading," Tyler explained. "They really stressed to her the importance of 'saying it now,' while she still had the chance." Each of those spirits had passed bearing the heavy regret of not saying what needed to be said to their loved ones before it was too late.

"She took this message in a really beautiful way," he said. "After our reading, she ended up recording a video to be played at her funeral, talking directly to a number of the people whom she knew would be in attendance." Heather also created a time capsule to be opened years after her death with personalized notes and mementos so that people could have new memories of her. She even went so far as to fill out birthday cards for her son every single year until he was forty, ensuring that every year he would be able to get a birthday greeting from his mom. "I think that speaks to the power of spirits to inspire us," said Tyler. "In this case, it was about making the most of the time that we have."

After many years of conducting readings that help people connect with lost loved ones, Tyler has gained knowledge from these spirits that informs how he lives his life. "My understanding of the ripple effect has really changed how I approach every action and every inaction," he said, referring to the notion that what we do every day, in a positive or negative way, reverberates throughout the physical and social world.

"The individuals I connect with in the afterlife tend to have a greater self-awareness of how everything they did and didn't do affected the greater collective," Tyler explained. "One of my most important takeaways from communicating with them is that we are like a drop of water and when we transition into the afterlife, we ultimately become part of a vast ocean of consciousness interconnected in ways we can't really grasp while we're here.

"That understanding has made me more mindful," he added. "When I see somebody in need, I am more inclined to think, you know, maybe I should stop and help, versus thinking, oh, somebody else will stop for them.... I've learned to better recognize opportunities to do good and try to take advantage of them when they present themselves."

You can call it karma or "what goes around comes around," or whatever you want, but like Tyler, I believe our actions in this life have a lasting impact that can extend into the afterlife. And because we have no idea when our time will come, we can't wait until the end to be a good person: pay it forward, say what needs to be said, and give back to your community. The ripple effect starts now.

A dear friend of mine, Bart Murrell, is living that philosophy as he grapples with illnesses that are threatening his life. At this point in his life, he is experiencing what he calls "cancer limbo." It's not the first time he's been up against the odds when it comes to his health.

For most of his time on Earth, Bart has had to overcome adversity. "Life to me was about survival," he said, having lost both his parents by the time he was nineteen. While his life's work has been performing, directing, dancing, and creating, he didn't find dance until he was twenty, a decade after most serious dancers have started, and he had to fight hard to make his way on the stage.

After years of struggle, Bart had finally gotten to a great place in his life, touring with national dance companies and sharing his life with his partner Antoine. But in 1990, they were both diagnosed with AIDS.

"I remember distinctly," he said. "My doctor started running water in the sink in his office. And he said, 'Do you see this water running into the drain? That's what your life is like, except the drain keeps on getting larger. Your time is running out. You've got about two years to live.' I remember leaning up against the wall in the doctor's office going, *Oh my god.* I was thirty-seven. I was coming into my prime as a dancer. I remember driving home and realizing I went through a red light because I had just heard that I was going to die. I had AIDS. Everybody who had AIDS died. I was numb."

More than 31,000 people died from AIDS in this country in 1990 alone. I find it hard to fathom, for numerous reasons, how he was able to process what was happening to him. He was living through a health crisis that was only getting worse. He had witnessed his once-healthy friends die in a matter of months. A diagnosis of AIDS in 1990 was considered a death sentence. How do you keep going after that? The weight of the fear and uncertainty had to have been crushing.

"I have always managed to make the best of a situation, to think my cup has always been three quarters full," he said. "I don't know where I got that from, but it's always been that way. It was at that point in time that I realized, 'Well, I'm just going to dance as long as I can and whatever happens, happens.'"

At that time, AZT was the preferred option for treatment, but the side effects were crippling: severe intestinal issues, damage to the immune system, terrible headaches, and insomnia. Bart took it; Antoine refused. Five years later, Bart's health was stabilizing, but Antoine passed away. Despite the heartbreaking loss, Bart continued to push forward. He focused on getting healthy while also doing what he loved. He danced, choreographed, worked on his craft, and kept himself busy. He didn't give up.

Then, in 2012, Bart was diagnosed with colon cancer. As always, he kept dancing and pushing forward. He went into remission for a time, but now the cancer has come back and metastasized. He says he's taking this one day at a time, and believes he's stronger at this point in his life than he was back in the early '90s.

"Of course, it's a big deal for everybody," he said, "but it really isn't."

I was a bit confused by this statement. How was it not a big deal? "Because it is what it is," Bart explained. "I was told that I had colon cancer. What am I going to do about it? I don't want to die, so I'm going to deal with it. I dealt with HIV and I'm going to deal with this. What can I do? Be healthy. Go forward, dancers, go forward. Live my life. I jump! I have always jumped forward.

"You have to deal with what life hands you with a sense of humor," Bart added. "I never let HIV stop me from dancing. I'm not going to let cancer stop me from living." Bart found a sense of comfort in his inner strength and in his relentless commitment to living and not letting a potentially life-threatening illness get in the way of his spiritual strength. There were moments in his journey when he could have given up but his connection to the universe around him elevated his way of thinking. As an artist he focused on his mission and purpose in life, which helped him through the toughest moments. He doesn't believe in an afterlife per se, though he does see a kind of continuation. "I think my energy goes back out into the universe to be reused," he said. This recycled energy, as a conglomerate of everyone and everything, came up in John E.L. Tenney's near-death experience as well. Bart's connection to his relationships in life and artistic passion in this world is preparing a place for him in the next.

"I remember one time after doing a performance I broke down crying backstage because I felt that was the first time I became one with the universe," he told me.

I know exactly what he means. On stage, there comes a moment when you are so energetically connected to the material and the audience that you completely disappear into the universe. You become one with everything and everyone. There is an exchange of energy from the audience to those on stage and back. It flows like a giant current and moves some to tears and goosebumps; sometimes an audience is so overcome people leap to their feet in applause. These kinds of moments, on or off stage, are the closest I will get to experiencing the sublime, a transcendent feeling of being connected to everything and everywhere at the same time.

This collective energy, which is repurposed over and over again, might be interpreted as reincarnation and past lives. I believe that both can occur and I have had a strange experience with the latter. Back before I was deep diving into the paranormal, I met a psychic who asked if she could give me a past life reading. At the time, I was young and I had little life experience. I lived in a place, like John, where I relied on myself alone for spiritual context, but when she asked if she could give me a reading I didn't say no. I was intrigued by the idea that she could give me some insight into the afterlife. She took my left hand with her right and held it palm facing up. Then placing her left hand on top, she took a deep breath and without any hesitation she said, "What's your obsession with the British flag?"

I had to pause for a second and tried to pull my hand away a little, but she held on tight. It was such a random thing to say—I hadn't given any indication that I liked a Union Jack design. I did, however, have a giant tapestry of the flag separating two parts of my dorm room in college. I also used to sew patches of the flag onto my jeans.

She continued, "You were called to Boston as your next place to settle in your journey because of this past life." She was right again; I had felt a tug to the city of Boston when I was choosing a college. When we visited, I was immediately in love. During my freshman year, I used to walk the streets around Faneuil Hall, exploring the old cobblestone roads, and visiting the oldest cemeteries in the country. "You were a British soldier, who was shot and left for dead during a winter of the Revolutionary War," the psychic said. Strangely it made complete sense to me, as if I had been told something I knew deep down all this time.

"Also," she added, "that's why your feet get cold first before anything else." She was spot on. I had never met this lady before in my life, she knew nothing about me, yet her reading was so precise.

That energy that Bart and John talk about recycling into someone or something else makes sense to me. She was picking up on that residue that was left over, which had influenced my own personal journey.

It's not just reincarnation into another human form that we hear stories about. After losing a loved one, many people speak about having relatives visit them, not in a ghostly way, but in different material forms. These aren't just regular moments but something that happens which seems completely bizarre. Birds seem to be the most common, but there have also been other animals that just appear out of nowhere, make a connection with people, and move on.

After my friend Casey passed, the day of his funeral, I went for a walk. Out of nowhere a monarch butterfly flew around his former sporting goods store where he worked, and I instantly knew it was Casey. I reached out my hand as if to say hello, and the butterfly descended from the sky and came directly to my finger, almost as if it was going to land.

"Hello, Casey," I said. It fluttered there at the tip of my finger, hovering so that I really was able to take in the moment, and then after an unusually long time it flew back across the street and up into the sky. Those who've had these types of experiences know how powerful they can be. It confirms for me that our energy is recycled in some way. Maybe not all of it, because again, there are spirits who remain as ghosts. But I am encouraged by the idea that we may return to the universe and in turn the universe returns to us.

We tend to think that paranormal investigators and psychics are our only conduit to the mysteries of the afterlife, but sometimes a person who is near death catches a glimpse of what is coming without any professional assistance. It happened in my own family.

Ben's grandmother Ruth Sumner passed away in 2017, at age ninety. I always loved Ruth. She knew how to put on some ruby-red lipstick and was generally the life of the party. She never shied away from a competitive game of UNO, and I never had so much fun at a casino than with her while she sat at her slots. In a word, she was, and still is, magnificent.

A few days after her ninetieth birthday, Ruth suffered a heart attack. My mother-in-law Wendy Elgin told me about the days afterward, just before she passed. When she had the cardiac event, they rushed her to the hospital, and while it wasn't her time yet, it was getting close. The doctors admitted her and made her as comfortable as possible, which wasn't easy but after a while Ruth relaxed into a state of peace. "One of us was always in the room with her," Wendy said. "My sister had just left the room and I wanted to go back in and talk to my mom. She was lying in the bed comfortably and was wide awake, and we started talking. Mid-sentence she stopped and she looked at me, and she said, 'You know, I can see right through your head.' I thought she was joking," Wendy added. "I said, 'You can, really? Well, what do you see?'"

"I see there's a church pew, and there's a man and a lady sitting in the church pew," Ruth responded, but she couldn't tell who the people were.

Wendy and her sisters speculated that perhaps it was Ruth's son and daughter who had died at birth, and maybe they were waiting for her. Or perhaps it was her mother and father who had passed years before her. I think the significance of seeing a church had to do with the fact that she was a religious person and held on to her faith all her life. Maybe the two figures sitting in the pew were there to guide her on the way. Maybe those were her two guardian angels. Just as there are opposites in nature, I believe there is the same balance of opposites in the spiritual world. Spirituality through life isn't one-directional. It ebbs and flows like the tides of the ocean. Where there is light there is dark, good and evil, yin and yang. I see these two spiritual beings as working together as a balance, to help people through this life. Maybe her guardians were waiting patiently for the time to come.

Ruth's lucid visions continued. "Mom was looking up at the ceiling and she lifted her arm and said 'Oh, here comes the train,'" Wendy said. "We all looked at each other like, 'What the hell, what train?' And then she said, 'Here it comes again.' I asked her what the train was for. She said, 'Well, don't worry, it's not my turn. I can't get on it yet.'"

Shortly after, in the same conversation, Ruth sat up in bed and said, "There's Eddie, I see him! He's on the train." None of the sisters knew who Eddie was. It wasn't until after Ruth's passing that they found out she had a cousin named Eddie who was the family favorite, who died during World War II. One of the strangest things, which I find fascinating, is that her family didn't know any of the names Ruth mentioned during these days. They were all unfamiliar and they made it a point to go through all of her old photos to see if they could match them up. Eddie was the only one they could corroborate.

Ruth called out the train one more time—the day after—and the same thing happened. She said that it wasn't her turn, and that she couldn't get on. But Wendy found comfort in these moments with her mom. They might seem weird, but to the family, they weren't. "They comforted us because we could tell that she was already partly passing over or getting ready, and this assured us there is another place where you go," Wendy said. "I think it helped all of us. I know it made our faith even stronger because of what we've experienced with our mom."

Faith had always been a guidepost for Ruth, and, in a way, I think she was deeply connected to everything around her during this moment. She didn't shy away from saying what she thought, she took every moment to be present if she could, and never showed any fear with what was happening and what she was seeing.

"We slept in her hospital room," Wendy said. "We always said goodnight to her, kissed her, told her we loved her. We'd sing songs and it got very quiet. All I could hear was her breathing. It was probably an hour, hour and a half later on her last night—I heard her voice and I woke up, and she was saying the Lord's Prayer. I didn't know if that was the end. But the next day, even though she was still breathing, she never woke up."

Ruth passed on the following day after advice from the nurse, who had worked at the hospital for quite some time. She told the sisters to leave the hospital, to go have lunch or just take a break, and let their mom be. Her thinking was if they were to leave their mom for a brief period, she would pass on her own.

Wendy and her sisters went and had a bite to eat then headed to their mom's apartment—there was a folder there labeled "church" that contained her wishes for her final preparations. They had already picked out what they wanted her to be buried in; when they opened the folder, there was a picture of Ruth. On the back of the photo, it said, "This is what I want to wear for my funeral." It was the same exact dress. Not even a minute later, Wendy's phone rang—it was the nurse saying that Ruth had passed.

The sisters let go, much like the case with Sue at the Lizzie Borden house, and Ruth was able to move on to her next journey.

Something similar happened on my side of the family, too. My mamaw, Betty Marie Irkard Taylor, passed in 2008 at age ninety-three—the kindest, sweetest lady who ever lived. She was always sitting outside waiting for us to arrive when we'd go for a visit, and her smile was so bright we could see it all the way down the end of her massively long driveway. Mamaw lived a long and amazing life, and when it was her time to journey on to the hereafter, her family—seven kids, ten grandkids, and ten great grandkids—was there to see her off. My mom, Sylvia, would keep me updated during Mamaw's hospital stay and had some really incredible moments with her that gave my mom hope that she would be at peace when the time came.

"This particular day, we were all sitting in her room talking to her and all of a sudden Mother started singing a spiritual hymn," she said. Mamaw had been in the hospital a few days and up until this moment she had not spoken a word. She was here, living, still breathing, but had not had any reaction or response for quite some time. A lot of my family was in the room during this time, and my mom recalled that everyone was so moved by what happened that you could hear a pin drop.

My aunt Wanda and her mother (my Grannie) were also there. "The hymn she sang was 'When We All Get to Heaven.' She said something about seeing Jesus. Mother and I looked at each other and said, 'She's ready to go to heaven!'"

The lyrics to the first part of that particular hymn read,

Sing the wondrous love of Jesus,
Sing His mercy and His grace;
In the mansions bright and blessed
He'll prepare for us a place.
When we all get to Heaven,
What a day of rejoicing that will be!
When we all see Jesus,
We'll sing and shout the victory!

I think Mamaw's singing was her way of preparing for what was coming next, and for finally reaching the place she had prayed about her whole life. My mom said she sang the entire song from beginning to end.

"We just sat there and listened and waited," she said. "Of course, we were all in tears by the time she got through singing. That's the last thing she ever said before she passed over; she never said anything else."

In a way, she set her own ship on a course to what was next. I don't know if she was consciously aware of singing or if it was in her spirit to do so, but she left this Earth shortly after. She made that choice on her own terms. "The doctor had already told us she didn't have long," my mom said. "I would go and visit her and I would read to her and talk to her. I just felt like I had a connection with her. What was so strange about it is that we wanted to be there with her when she passed and the nurses came in and said, we need to give Mother a bath, and asked us to go down the hall and wait until they were through."

Not even ten minutes later, Mamaw was gone. "I went back to the room because I saw the nurses going back and forth across the hall. I went through the door and Mother was laying there. The nurse looked up at me and I said, 'She's gone.' And she said, 'Yes ma'am, she's gone.'

"'Yeah,' I said to my mother, 'we went down the hall! We wanted to be in the room with you, but you weren't gonna let us do that.' She was gonna go on her own terms. She was fierce and she just wanted to make sure we were protected. She didn't want her children to see her die."

Just like Ben's grandmother Ruth, Mamaw waited until her children were no longer there to make her transition. My mom believes it was because she was always very protective of her children. They both had strong motherly instincts, always aware when their children were in need. The family was grieving already. Once their energy was out of the room, she felt the shift, and let go, knowing that her work in this life was done.

At the end of my life, if I am fortunate enough, I will let go of this world by moving forward, pushing through, jumping. Yes, it can be scary, but I will try to stay strong for others that I want to protect and for myself. Being afraid of what's to come gets in the way of living in the here and now.

My friend Bart, who has faced the fear of the unknown all his life, says it best: "Be fearless. I can't say it enough. Be fearless. I think I was always insecure and I finally learned that fear is false evidence appearing as real." In the past few years, Bart has taken up bungee jumping and parasailing in beautiful exotic places he's always dreamed of traveling—he grasps the concept of "No day but today," that famous lyric from the musical RENT, like no one I have ever met. He says it helps him conquer fear in everyday life.

"Fear," he says, "is just another emotion that I can use to create and survive."

I am fully aware that this is easier said than done. None of us are alone in the journey into the unknown. Everyone who has gone before us has paved a way, and prepared a place for those yet to board that train. The acceptance or rejection of what's next is up to each individual. The paths we take are singular and precious. We each get to a place of understanding in our own time and I personally lean on the advice of those in the afterlife, to help us better understand what's to come.

But for you and I, here and now, this beautiful world is here for us to feel alive in, and anything we can do to connect deeper to it should be a priority. Living in the moment, embracing each day, saying what needs to be said now and not waiting. Saying "I love you" to those who matter. All of the things that aren't too late for us to accomplish. We are not promised tomorrow but we are here today. Fight those fears and push beyond your own spiritual constraints. Jump.

The end. The beginning.

Afterword

This book is an exploration into my own personal and philosophical ideas about the afterlife, which have taken my entire life to compile. But I will be totally honest with you: by the time you read this, those ideas will probably be different—or at least, will have evolved. I learn by experience and observation, so at this moment in my spiritual journey I can only share what I know and understand up to this point. The one thing I know for certain is that there is more to discover.

While I am not an actual therapist and can't give medical advice, in the past, Amy and I have been called therapists for ghosts. It makes sense: we're offering comfort to the non-living and trying to help them by better understanding their circumstances. In return, they teach me so much about my own existence and life on this earth. For me, paranormal research is an avenue to understanding what's beyond this world.

I have spent my life questioning everything and making my own choices as to what to believe, looking at those ideas and seeing how they may or may not influence my personal spiritual and psychological beliefs. My hope is that's what you do, too, especially when it comes to questioning every idea and thought in this book. Take them in, and then see if they fit with your own beliefs and passions. Whether you agree with everything or not, your exploration might just broaden your own spiritual journey. Most importantly, have faith in the practice, understanding, and outcomes of your own life experiences. Take what you can from this book, and find ways to expand your own way of thinking about grief and death. Find comfort in the uncomfortable and revel in positive progress. The more we question and dive deeper into our own personal beliefs, the more we can experience a change in the way we fear the unexplainable.

If you've come to this book because you're grieving or coping with loss, I hope you find a way to use the stories and theories in these pages to propel your own journey. I can't tell you how to grieve and there is no magical cure to ease your pain, but sometimes we need a little help to keep us going to a new thought or idea, continuing our own personal healing.

A recurring theme from the other side is to be in the moment and focus on connection and relationships. This idea includes both the living and the dead. I believe that if you want to talk to a friend or loved one who has passed, just do it. Talk to them, meditate, or pray and tell them how you feel, or even say it out loud. Say their name three times in a row. Ask them to help you through the process—because if there's anything that can be learned from this book is that communication between the living and the dead can happen. Celebrate their life. Continue to honor them on special occasions. Focus on the joy and love that you experienced while they were alive. We have been blessed by the ones we care so deeply for in life and we can carry that with us always.

We cannot escape grief or loss. Death is really the only guaranteed event in life, but we can ease each other's burden by sharing our collective experiences with one another. Connecting with the living world around us is just another way of honoring and respecting the dead. We learn from those who are here and those who have passed, and we can let those teachings guide us to a better understanding of our own journey. Those who have gone before are paving the way for those yet to come.

They sometimes have very little to say, but when they do speak we should listen. We are lucky to receive any small dose of wisdom they have gained by moving through the veil. The biggest thing to realize is that we are all one, even before we cross over. We are connected, and the ripple effects from our actions or inactions have consequences far beyond ourselves.

For me, looking for ghosts has made me a more spiritual person. I never could have imagined how looking for ghosts would force me to delve into deeper conversations about life, death, and what comes next. With each new supernatural encounter, I am encouraged by the idea that our essence will still live on somewhere after this life. However, that doesn't change the fact that I sometimes still experience fear and uncertainty around the idea of death. I love my life and I want to absorb what this world has to offer. I want to see, hear, touch, smell, love, breath, cry, sing, and connect, to everything and everyone.

Now, my uncertainty around death stems from the fear of missing out. I sometimes think about milestones that are decades away and I pray that I reach those. My next spiritual journey is to embrace the here and now, while I have it, and live life to the fullest. "No day but today," forever and always.

Never stop dreaming. Never stop questioning. Never get old in your ways. There is always so much more to learn. Life is for living, learning, and having adventures. The afterlife is for what comes next. Find comfort in asking, "What if?" As Hamlet says after he encounters the ghost of his deceased father, "There are more things in heaven and earth, Horatio, than are dreamt of in your philosophy." Indeed, there are. Embrace the unknown and what comes next.

Acknowledgments

This book has been a labor of love and I couldn't have completed this journey without the help of many of my friends, family members, and colleagues who shared their stories, gave their insights, and offered their support when I needed it the most. Some simply answered their phones, checked on how I was progressing, made me a cocktail, or just sent a text to say, "You got this." I cannot ever thank you enough.

To my husband Ben, the support and unwavering love you have shown during this process was simply breathtaking. I couldn't have done it without you. Thank you for being there for me throughout. The care that you have shown me, so that I could fulfill the dream of writing my first book, is something I can never repay. However, I will try. I revel in the knowledge that in the coming years, whatever projects we dream up, we will be each other's biggest advocate. I would not want to be on this journey with anyone else and I know with you by my side, we can achieve everything we have ever wanted. I cannot wait for you to say, "Have you written anything today?" a thousand times over. I love you with all my heart.

Julie Tremaine, the one who helped me find my thoughts, balanced my ideas, and pushed me further than anyone has before. I thank you. Your guidance, edits, and knowledge were an entire AP English Literature course in the span of a few months. Thank you for making me laugh and finding the levity when I was pulling my hair out. You are one of a kind.

Thank you to my family who shared their personal stories, showed their support and encouragement, and gave me unconditional love every minute. There is something to be said for someone being there for you, even late at night, so that I could pick your brain or have you elaborate on a story. Special shout-outs to my aunts Wanda Berry and Rita Berry Seaton, whose stories came out of pure coincidence, upon hearing of my book, one autumn evening in Vermont. So much love to my mom and dad, Sylvia and Junior Berry, who could never run out of stories to tell and with whom I continue to have new adventures. Get ready for the memoir.

To my mother-in-law Wendy Elgin, who's always been so supportive. Thank you for sharing Ruth's moments and for allowing me to include her in one of the most important chapters.

To Amy Bruni, without whom I would not be where I am today. My journey, up to this moment in my life, isn't a singular one. Your friendship has shaped my existence. I don't think it was mere chance that our lives crossed paths and I will never take that for granted. We are family, not simply friends, and our journey in this life gets better with age like a fine California Chardonnay. May we continue to explore the unknown together until we are pushing each other around in wheelchairs in abandoned haunted buildings. I can't wait for new and magical experiences. To more vacations and taking the world by storm. Thanks Champagne!

To friends and collogues, who gave of their time and expertise to make this book the best it can be. I have always looked to those I respect, who have more knowledge on certain topics, so that I may grow, not only as a researcher, but as a human being. I am in awe of your talents and support.

Chip Coffey, I love you ma'am! You have always been so supportive and, ever since we first met, you have treated Ben and me as family. This is what I love about you, among many other things. Thank you for your time and wisdom.

John E.L. Tenney, I love you. You are the most interesting paranormal man in the world and I can't wait for all of us to be one and everyone all at once forever and ever. Thank you for supporting me and constantly making me think deeper and explore further. Your kindness is worn not only on your sleeve but it emanates from your entire spirit. You are an original.

Greg and Dana Newkirk, there are no words to show my appreciation but I will try. Thank you both for showing love always and never shying away from your beliefs, feelings, and theories. You push everyone around you to be better and think deeper. Without your work and friendship, I would not be the person I am today. My love and gratitude are unwavering. I am so honored to call you family.

Steve Gonsalves, thank you for your time and dedication to this project. You have always been my biggest supporter and stood in my corner so many times, even when the odds were set against me. I love you. I am so happy that we can share in each other's successes and I appreciate our mutual love for Broadway musicals more than you will ever know. Cheers to you and your continued success.

Sarah Coombs, thank you for sharing your passions and gifts with the world. You have always been so kind to me, and the joy you share with the world has no boundaries.

To my new friend Tyler Henry. You are one of a kind, and you radiate so much love and light. May it shine forever and always.

Thank you for sharing your stories, wisdom, and conversation with me. I can't wait to join you on a paranormal investigation.

Thank you to my dear friend Kathy Kelly, without whom I would be a less interesting person. Thank you for sharing your stories and for being such a great friend, mentor, and inspiration. I am along for whatever journey you are leading and cannot wait to see where it will take us.

Thank you to Matt Arnold, whose wisdom and knowledge opened my eyes to my own religious upbringing through a deeper understanding of biblical texts.

To those who gave their time and energy to telling their story again. Who trusted me, with precious memories, so I could better understand your own paranormal and emotional history. Your bravery and love helped me unlock new ideas, not only for this book but within myself. Thank you for being so open about your grief, loss, and ghostly encounters so that others can learn and grow in their own spiritual journeys. I have never been more humbled by your generosity: Kate Pazakis, Missy Valvo, Melissa Daniel, Yvette Rovira, Sharon Webb, Linda DeCicco, and Sandy Donati. May this book be in memory of those whose stories you shared. May this be a way that, even decades from now, they will not be forgotten. Love and light, always.

Gretchen Young, my editor, who when starting her own publishing house, Regalo Press, picked my book to be one of the first. Your curiosity and support have pushed this book further than I could have imagined. Here's to many more partnerships and publications! I applaud your support of charitable organizations through publication.

Bill Stankey, my manager, who's been by my side over these last nine years. Thank you for pushing me and always believing in me, helping me realize my own potential and self-worth.

Acknowledgments

To Marc Chamlin for keeping it legal and for Mary Lalli, whose support and emails I always look forward to. There is no "I" in team and you two are shining examples.

Last but not least to all of my followers, fans, and supporters, including those who may be finding this book and never knew me before. Your support means so much to me and I would not be able to do what I love to do without you.

To those fans who watched every episode of *Kindred Spirits* and transcribed all of the "spirit communication" question and answer sessions and dialogue, so that I would have more time to write, you are a blessing: Mike Archer, Sara Casey, Shayla Connell, Christine Duckels, Samantha Jackson, Jill Johnston, and Amy "marshmallow chair" Shields. Thank you so very much.

Finally, to my chihuahua Cheeto Burrito BerryMeyer. Sun-pig. I know losing your sister Maria Conchita wasn't easy on you, but I learned so much from your resilience. You love me and Ben unconditionally and when we were lost in deep grief you were there to comfort us, despite your own. Just as I love your sister, I will love you forever and always.